Taking Giving Seriously

Paul G. Schervish

and

Obie Benz

Peggy Dulany

Thomas B. Murphy

Stanley Salett

Edited by Patricia Dean

Indiana University
Center on Philanthropy

Indiana University - Purdue University
Indianapolis

Library of Congress Catalog Card Number: 93-80296

ISBN 1-884354-00-9

Book layout and design by Sam Mattes.

TABLE OF CONTENTS

ACKNOWLEDGMENTS

The editor thanks the authors for their cooperation throughout the publication process. Their support lightened the editorial burden considerably.

Thanks go also to all of the participants in the Indiana University Center on Philanthropy's "Taking Giving Seriously" seminar, who lent the weight of firsthand experience to this publication. Equally valuable was the material contributed by subjects of a Boston College study of wealthy donors, which was used here as a core resource in two chapters authored by Paul G. Schervish.

Two figures who were central to this project from inception to conclusion are Robert L. Payton, former executive director of the Indiana University Center on Philanthropy, and Dwight F. Burlingame, director of academic programs and research at the Center on Philanthropy.

Special appreciation goes to Lois Sherman for professional managing of the publication process, to Sam Mattes for expert handling of text and design, and to Center on Philanthropy staff for providing the essential support to carry this publication through.

Finally, the Lilly Endowment, in providing crucial support for this project, has exhibited once again that it "takes giving seriously."

INTRODUCTION

Patricia Dean

For those without it, wealth may appear to be an unmitigated blessing, opening the door to endless opportunities. For those with wealth, it may be as much burden as blessing, bringing opportunity certainly, but obligation as well. Accepting both the obligations and the opportunities of wealth, the wealthy individuals represented in this anthology have become philanthropists. In so doing, they have chosen to do more than simply give money to philanthropic causes. They have accepted also an obligation to consider seriously the uses to which their money might be put, because—as they say repeatedly—they want to "make a difference." But determining what will make a difference is not easy. As Obie Benz points out, "It is difficult to give money away well and there will inevitably be a long learning process." It is our hope that the wisdom here presented, by experienced philanthropists and scholars of philanthropy, may help others who are engaged in that learning process.

The origins of this anthology lie in a seminar and a research project. All of the contributors to this volume participated in "Taking Giving Seriously: The Responsibilities and Opportunities of Wealth," a seminar sponsored by the Indiana University Center on Philanthropy in November, 1991. And a study of 130 wealthy individuals conducted by Boston College provided much of the material for the two essays by Paul Schervish.

The intent of the "Taking Giving Seriously" seminar was to provide an opportunity for wealthy donors to reflect on their philanthropic histories and philosophies, to share their reflections with an audience of their peers, and to discuss ways to encourage philanthropy in this generation and the next. This anthology has similar intentions.

Three of the chapters in this anthology—those by Thomas Murphy, Obie Benz, and Peggy Dulany—present personal, anecdotal material drawn from the life histories of the authors. The other three chapters—two by Paul Schervish and one by Stanley Salett—present a more comprehensive picture of the attitudes and practices of wealthy donors.

The first personal perspective comes from Thomas B. Murphy, who, like Obie Benz, is impressed with the learning required to do philanthropy well. In his essay, Murphy conveys the conclusions he has reached after ten years as an active philanthropist, protesting that he still has much to learn. Some of that learning apparently will come from further experimentation with giving, because, as he notes, there is no ordered body of knowledge, "no 'do-it-yourself kit' for philanthropy, to provide neophytes with sound, detailed information." He also finds unsatisfactory the methods that are available to measure the effects of one's philanthropic efforts. Despite the difficulties encountered in practicing philanthropy, Murphy is a true believer in its potential to do good for those in need and in its satisfactions for benefactors. A vigorous advocate, he says that participating in philanthropy offers "a measure of happiness that cannot be achieved in any other way...," and he urges "all to become participants" in the philanthropic enterprise.

In the first of his two essays in this anthology, Paul Schervish summarizes the themes that emerged in the seminar discussions. Those themes are related to decisions that donors are compelled to make when they choose to become involved in philanthropy—issues such as how to make their philanthropy effective; how to make it expressive of their own values and giving styles; how to foster giving by others, including their own children; and how philanthropic identities are developed. He develops the last theme at some length.

Defining philanthropy as "an identity in which care for others becomes a vocation," Schervish presents a list of six factors he finds to be typical in the personal histories of philanthropists. As an example of how the factors actually operate, Schervish concludes this essay with excerpts from an interview with one of the 130 wealthy donors in the Boston College study.

In the next two chapters, authors Obie Benz and Peggy Dulany speak from their perspective as wealthy donors. Their narratives about having and sharing wealth exhibit clearly the two sides of philanthropy—its obligations and its opportunities. Benz and Dulany also expose a dark side of wealth in their discussions of the difficulties it creates in human relations; Benz even suggests that, in certain respects, children raised in wealthy families may be deprived. In an effort to live a more "normal" life, Dulany ceased to use her famous family name, and Benz went through a period of hiding his wealth from all but a few close friends. Acutely conscious of the disparities caused by wealth, both have chosen to perceive their wealth as an obligation to advance the common good and have founded organizations to do just that. It may be, as Dulany asserts in her own case, that social conscience is rooted in an "early consciousness of something being different."

Stanley Salett's objective is to expand giving by wealthy individuals and families. He argues that more attention should be paid to private wealth as a philanthropic resource, because "the largest potential growth in philanthropy in the next two decades is likely to come from individuals and families." Part of the explanation for this fact is that a $6.8 trillion dollar intergenerational transfer of wealth will occur during that period. Salett's barrage of statistics generates a picture of a concentration of wealth held by a small group of people, many of whom have unimpressive philanthropic records. Not wanting to wait for history to reveal just how philanthropic the next generation will be, Salett prefers to set about immediately turning "the wealthiest segment of that generation toward greater giving." It is, he says, "a task worthy of our best organized and systematic efforts."

The closing chapter in the anthology is a second essay by Paul Schervish, this time a theoretical piece advancing a definition of philanthropy that makes the virtue of charity central to philanthropy. In this move, Schervish reunites the practice of philanthropy with its semantic roots. Placing charity at the center of the philanthropic relation means that the boundaries of self-interest will be extended to encompass the interests of others. The resulting "communion of interests" bears rewards which, as Thomas Murphy says, "cannot be described; they must be experienced."

THE WISDOM OF PHILANTHROPY

Thomas B. Murphy

In the early 1980s, my family and business situation permitted me not only to think about philanthropy but to actively pursue some philanthropic initiatives. As an aspiring and inexperienced philanthropist, I had much to learn. After ten years I still do.

In this essay, I attempt to set forth some of what I have observed, some of what I have learned, and some conclusions I have reached. Much of what I observed, learned, and concluded is personal, subjective, and probably not transferable. It is this uniqueness of the philanthropic experience that holds such promise, not only for those who choose to become involved but for society as a whole.

This essay will discuss some unique characteristics of philanthropy, the wisdom of philanthropy for individuals, the wisdom of philanthropy for society, and the potential of philanthropy.

Some Unique Characteristics of Philanthropy

Philanthropy has three unique characteristics that indicate the vast, underdeveloped potential for philanthropic activity.

The first concerns the boundaries of the field; it is essentially a field that knows no boundaries. Individuals embarking on an individual philanthropic journey can discover worthy projects in areas as near as their own backyard or as distant as some remote corner of the earth. Neither the type of project nor the mode of engagement is limited. One may initiate a project or join with others to support an existing project within one's area of interest or in an entirely new and different area.

The second differentiating characteristic of philanthropy concerns the way philanthropy differs from the sciences and professions, each of which is defined by an ordered body of knowledge. The body of knowledge related to philanthropy, while growing rapidly, is still in the embryonic stage; it is inadequate and often inaccessible. There is no "do-it-yourself kit" for philanthropy, to provide neophytes with sound, detailed information.

The third characteristic deals with standards or measures of performance, which for philanthropy appear to be absent. There is no adequate measure to judge the success or failure of a particular philanthropic initiative. The scope and variety of philanthropic projects suggest why such standards do not now exist, but this fact does not negate the need. It is unfortunate that the available data, from both governmental and private sources, reveal with decimal point accuracy the number of dollars applied to philanthropic purposes, but do not measure, either quantitatively or qualitatively, the effects of the application of these resources. It is the very essence of fund accounting (the prescribed accounting method for foundations and that used by government) to record, as the final entry for a given expenditure, the purpose for which the funds were expended. This method contrasts with accounting in the world of commerce, in which the beginning entry records the purpose and the final entry what happened as the result of the beginning entry.

Measuring the effectiveness of projects to improve the quality of life, as with the symphony or art exhibits, requires techniques different from measuring the results of a project to develop the intellectual capacity of children. Yet measures can be developed for these and other anticipated results of philanthropic initiatives. Such is the promise and challenge of philanthropy.

The Wisdom of Philanthropy for Individuals

Aristotle chided us to look for happiness not in things nor in the applause of other men but in wisdom, which for him meant "wise choice." For those with redundant resources—resources over and above those needed to meet their own needs and those of their families—the choice to devote some of their resources (time and money) to philanthropic activity can, if wisely conceived and executed, provide the donor a measure of happiness that cannot be achieved in any other way, and one that cannot be described but must be experienced.

The benefit that accrues to donors emanates from the intrinsic dimension of philanthropic activity as opposed to the extrinsic. The intrinsic benefits flow from the relationship between the philanthropic activity and the donor, that is, the satisfaction—and on occasion the exhilaration—that accompanies bringing about a worthwhile result. The extrinsic benefits are those that flow with the resources applied, as in the granting of funds for a scholarship to a deserving student. In this case, the extrinsic benefit is the funds that create an educational opportunity; the intrinsic dimension, which can be positive or negative, depends on the success of the student. The benefit is positive if the student graduates, negative if the student flunks out.

The Wisdom of Philanthropy for Society

From the perspective of society, philanthropy is indeed a wise choice. It provides a solution to the problem of inequities in the distribution of wealth. In the United States, the rate of growth of wealth is greater than the rate of growth of the population, a condition favorable for improvements in the quality of life. While market-oriented economies have proven to be superior for the creation of wealth, they do not distribute wealth uniformly over the population. Command economies, on the other hand, exhibit superiorities in distributing wealth but have been inadequate in creating wealth. Real world systems, such as in the United States and other industrialized economies, incorporate elements of each and differ from their theoretical constructs primarily in the degree to which emphasis is placed upon wealth creation and wealth redistribution. Within the United States, which clearly favors wealth creation, the emphasis on redistribution has varied over time.

That some redistribution is necessary is a given. Too little is inequitable. Too much retards economic growth. Voluntary redistribution (i.e., philanthropy) is uniquely equipped to operate in the median between the too little and the too much.

There are two ways, government assistance and private philanthropy, in which these harmful side effects can be mitigated. A successful response requires the use of each in the right proportion. Each is clearly imbedded in the system in ways that make their elimination virtually impossible as well as unwise, since each deals with a dimension of the problem that the other is ill-equipped to handle.

Government focuses on the effects that impact large segments of the population and that require the mobilization of huge resources. Private philanthropy focuses on the effects that impact smaller segments of the population and that require the commitment of more modest resources. A further distinction is that philanthropy can respond to problems and opportunities in a more flexible and timely manner than can the bureaucratic apparatus of government.

The necessity for private philanthropy arises from the fact that our economy is not one big market but thousands of small markets, each with its own supply and demand relationships, each being continually impacted by technological changes and supply/demand changes at home and abroad, each causing dynamic changes and dislocation that are as different as the events that caused them. No one person or organization is capable of monitoring this kaleidoscopic pattern, much less responding to it. Within this pattern are opportunities for the philanthropic impulse to vent itself through flexible methodologies, varying with and fitted to the opportunity.

Resources held in common, as in government, are allocated in a manner reflective of that amalgamation of interests necessary to achieve a consensus in a democracy. Such allocations, by necessity, contain within themselves the multiple objectives required to develop the consensus, a situation that results in a diffusion of the resources over the multiple objectives. In contrast, philanthropic initiatives, being voluntary and involving private property, can pursue single objectives with a singularity of purpose.

The Potential of Philanthropy

As this volume goes to print, the opportunities for constructive philanthropy that will both enhance the quality of human life and build human society have never been greater. The wealth-generating capacity of democratic capitalism has produced and distributed the resources to address these opportunities. Whether or not the enormous potential for successful private philanthropy will be translated into actual results is yet to be determined. Much of philanthropy's potential resides with the wealthy, who are financially, temporally, and psychologically positioned to address the limitless opportunities for philanthropy and to effect meaningful philanthropic outcomes.

While the potential for philanthropy has existed since the beginning of history, what has changed is the capacity of people to be philanthropic. More and more individuals, particularly in the United States, which has well over a million millionaires, have achieved levels of financial security over and above their needs and those of their families.

In the pages of this volume are the thoughts and recorded deeds of some who have not only "taken giving seriously" but have, in fact, brought about meaningful outcomes. The subject matter of this book—"taking giving seriously"—is drawn from the conversations and the biographies of people who have put into practice their own philanthropic principles. It is not only indicative of what *can* be done but what actually *has* been done.

Each individual occupies a moving seat on the stage of life. From this seat, one can choose to be a passive observer or an active participant in the unfolding scene. The enormous diversity of opportunities in the philanthropic arena beckons all to become participants—to move down from the grandstand to the playing field—to enter the fray—to succeed or fail—to win or lose—but, above all, to participate to the extent of one's ability. To those who elect to play, I can assure you, as can so many others who have elected to play, that the successes of philanthropy are of a different and higher order than those experienced in the world of commerce. They cannot be described; they must be experienced.

TAKING GIVING SERIOUSLY

Paul G. Schervish

This essay explores what it means to take giving seriously—to establish a philanthropic identity—and examines the various factors that lead wealthy individuals to form such an identity. My purpose is to provide a framework for understanding the discussions that took place at the conference "Taking Giving Seriously: The Responsibilities and Opportunities of Wealth." The conference was sponsored by the Indiana University Center on Philanthropy, at Indiana University-Purdue University at Indianapolis, on November 7 and 8, 1991. It brought together committed wealthy donors, foundation officers, and persons engaged in philanthropic research and administration, for discussions about issues surrounding the giving behavior of the wealthy—issues of motivation, values, recognition, family, decision-making, privacy, and social agenda. It was spurred in part by the fact that over the next two decades approximately one million individuals will receive inheritances of at least $1 million. The question, as Fred[1] puts it so well, is "How do we tap into this great intergenerational transfer?"

The conference was, in a way, an experimental effort. By providing a forum for wealthy individuals from various backgrounds to share their ideas and experiences with their peers, the conference planners hoped to develop a model for similar kinds of gatherings throughout the country. Such meetings would focus on how generous giving is fostered among the wealthy, how the large number of wealthy individuals not actively dedicated to philanthropy may be encouraged to become serious givers, and how the heirs of the current generation of wealthy individuals may be inspired to participate actively in charity.

The central argument running through this report is straightforward. To speak about "taking giving seriously" is to speak about philanthropy becoming an identity. To say that one has a philanthropic identity means that one's moral biography is shaped in large measure by devotion to the quantity and quality of one's charity. In discussing this topic, I draw on the transcribed notes from the conference sessions as well as on the 130 interviews with millionaires that were conducted as part of the *Study on Wealth and Philanthropy* at Boston College over the past several years.[2]

I begin by examining the discussions that took place during the conference.[3] From my point of view, the fundamental message of the conference is that philanthropy is an identity in which care for others becomes a vocation. Given this stress on philanthropy as identity, it is natural to ask what factors contribute to creating such a self-conception. I note six mobilizing factors: a community of participation; a framework of consciousness; a person or an experience in one's youth; mediating persons or organizations; a set of intrinsic and extrinsic rewards; and the presence of disposable resources.

In the second section I propose a *definition of philanthropy* as a social relation, indicating how it should be distinguished from commercial and political relations. Next, I examine the centrality of the *virtue of charity* in understanding philanthropy as a *moral identity* in which one links, rather than counterposes, love of self and love of neighbor. In conclusion, I examine a series of issues raised during the conference and in this paper that have to do specifically with inducing a deeper commitment to philanthropy among the current generation of wealthy people and instilling a philanthropic identity in the next generation.

PHILANTHROPY AS MORAL IDENTITY

Philanthropy is apparently so highly personalized for wealthy donors that their views tend to be based on their own experiences or the experiences of those in a close circle of family and friends. As a result, whatever principles about wealth and philanthropy the conference participants tender are offered as reflecting their personal predispositions, predilections, and politics. In no session do the participants seek to formulate anything approaching a consensus. Nevertheless, the sessions do reveal an important "subtext," or story behind the story, to which the participants subscribe almost universally. This is that philanthropy, when carried out at the level of intensity evinced by the conference participants, is more intimately connected to personal issues of moral identity than to abstract doctrine. The participants, even when asserting general principles, derive their views *a posteriori* from experience rather than *a priori* from theory. For every question the answer is ultimately, "it depends." It depends on what individual philanthropists wish to accomplish in regard to a specific cause *as well as* in regard to their money, their families, and themselves. Before turning to the broader theme of philanthropy as identity, I want to summarize the seven themes I found in the discussions.

Project Evaluation and Self-Evaluation

"Foundation work," comments one foundation executive, "is the only job where you can do a lousy job and still have money for the next year." This remark can be read cynically as a commentary on the potential lack of accountability in philanthropic funding. But the intention of this experienced foundation official was to emphasize the difficulty in determining whether philanthropic contributions achieve their purpose and whether, in fact, such efforts are valid in the first place. Every philanthropist and foundation professional must eventually give some consideration to these issues. As for the conference participants, their common concern was how to judge if an individual, organization, project, or cause is truly needy and worthy of support. And if it is, will the person or organization be effective in carrying out the goals? What constitutes such effectiveness? And how can it be measured?

Individual donors and representatives of foundations agree that similarities exist between philanthropic and for-profit ventures in the application of resources to achieve outcomes. But they also recognize, along with Jerry, that the major difference for philanthropy is the constant struggle "to measure performance when you don't have a profit structure." What Bill says—"It's harder to give well than to raise money well"—is echoed by Charles, who says, "it is easier to make money intelligently than to give it away intelligently." The reason, explains Charles, is that "in the business world, one allocates resources to achieve a particular goal: the highest rate of return. This is clear-cut and measurable. But in the philanthropic world it is harder to determine such a clear goal, and so the tendency is to measure not the results of one's contributions but simply the amount of dollars given. We need to focus on what has been accomplished in order to determine the efficient use of philanthropic resources. We need some methodology, based on probability theory, for measuring different outputs for results." Charles does not offer a specific solution to this measurement problem, but he articulates the problem well: "Philanthropy is too often like government in that it accounts for dollars spent, but that's where it ends. In fact, it should start there," because in philanthropy, in contrast to business, "money is not the end but the beginning" of the productive process.

Given the problem of measuring outcomes in philanthropy, the variation among participants about how and when to evaluate philanthropy is hardly surprising. For some, any evaluation is ultimately a matter of intuition. Carl, for example, says "self- trust is the most important guiding principle" in any evaluation because "[you] need a keen eye toward unintended consequences." Similarly, Gary sees "real practicality to evaluation but it is hard to tell on the surface. Thus there is need for an intuitive understanding, in dialogue with a grantee, that lets you know the grant was helpful. In the philanthropic world it is let the buyer trust *(credat emptor)*, while in the entrepreneurial world it is let the buyer beware *(caveat emptor)*." Bob concurs that evaluation of a project is a matter of discerning "how it feels, how it looks, and how it works. You have to have a feeling for it." Others stress a process in which the grantee is directly involved in determining the criteria of evaluation. "The most helpful thing," declares Patrick, "is to ask the grantee what he expects to accomplish and compare that with what actually happens."

Participants disagreed about the specificity and the timetable of any evaluation. Most described a philosophy of evaluation according to which individual projects would be evaluated regularly for their short-term accomplishments. However, Bob suggests that philanthropists should "help as many projects as possible and look again ten years later." This coincides with the view of Donald, who says "I'm a cause-oriented person; keep your eye on the big picture, rather than specific projects."

Some philanthropists think that if recipients are selected on the basis of leadership, further evaluation is not necessary. However, Donald thinks that "small foundations are impressed too often by one charismatic leader instead of evaluating the team of an organization. You really need to look at the organization as a whole." For Jim, "personal involvement of the donor is important" in the form of site visits, while for Earl another criterion is whether the recipient is capable of asking for and obtaining matching funds. Making a grant "contingent on matching dollars," he maintains, "is a good way to test whether an idea is good or not. What others give is just one factor—but an important one—of whether or not we give." Finally, others use the relative proportion of administrative overhead to program expenditures as a norm for evaluating whether to contribute.

Ultimately, the desire for evaluation of performance is not motivated mainly by a concern for control nor by a quest for technical measurement, although some donors seem to demonstrate such concerns. Several insist on keeping a close watch on their philanthropic investments and some desire a more stringent accounting of results than do their colleagues, but the major concern is not whether others are doing the right thing with the philanthropist's money. Rather it is whether the philanthropists themselves are doing the right thing. The former consideration may be a measure of the latter, but the underlying theme is that self-evaluation is the driving force behind the quest for evaluation and measurement. "It clearly goes beyond just writing checks; it touches the profound purpose-of-life questions," reflects Kevin. Charles concurs. "If you're applying resources in a certain way, then you use a creative way to apply them. If you want to be effective in real change, you must go beyond writing checks. Money is just one variable affecting outcomes, sometimes the least important, although we tend to see it as the most important—as *the* answer. But the key is mission and goals. Then you can see resources as the means needed to accomplish doable, worthwhile objectives." One must "ask people what they want," Charles insists, so that "philanthropy can help them reach objectives." Such a perspective does not come automatically with wealth: "You have to learn it; it is a whole new skill."

Philanthropists may be more or less adept at "letting go" of their money and trusting the recipients to make good use of a contribution. But whether they call for more or less direct scrutiny of the effectiveness of their donations, or have a shorter or longer timeline for evaluation, or want more or less personal involvement in the evaluation, those who take giving seriously take evaluation seriously. And they take evaluation seriously because, in that ever-recurring phrase, they want "to make a difference." They are identified with, rather than indifferent to, their philanthropic efforts, especially those they personally initiate, contribute to substantially, contribute their own time to, or feel to be crucial for social welfare. In every instance, evaluation of a project's anticipated worth and ultimate effectiveness always implies an equally careful self-evaluation.

Administration of Philanthropy

In addition to considerations about evaluation, serious giving requires reflection about how to administer one's philanthropy. Is it better to administer one's giving personally or to do so through a foundation? If the latter, then is it better to hire a professional staff for one's private foundation or to channel giving through a community foundation?

The title of the conference session, "How do you decide whom to trust with your wealth and with your values?," appropriately summarizes the key issues underlying the choice of an organizational strategy, for, indeed, values and the use of money are intimately related. The gospel is as correct in stating that "where your treasure is, there shall your heart be also," as is social science in asserting the reverse, that where your heart is, there shall your treasure be also.

None of the participants distinguishes between direct personal giving and the creation of a personal foundation as a legal form for personal giving. For all practical purposes, both personal giving and giving through a so-called "checkbook foundation" are considered forms of direct personal giving. The discussion revolves mainly around the extent to which one should use the assistance of professionals in managing major philanthropic efforts. Some emphasize the individual philanthropist's initiative and supervision. For Carl, as we have heard, "self-trust is the most important guiding principle" and should not be throttled by giving over one's judgment to others. Others such as Donald think that professionals "raise the level of performance because they're trained to do the job" and know more about it. Bill concurs that "it's harder to give well than to raise money well; for that reason you need a staff." Because of the complexities of administration and evaluation as well as the limits of time, Jim counsels, "At some point you must turn your philanthropy over to professionals."

Conversation about how to administer funds can be summarized under three rubrics: disadvantages of using a foundation, advantages of doing so, and advantages of a community foundation over a private foundation.

Disadvantages of carrying out one's giving through a foundation include the economic overhead of running a foundation; the distractions of administrative obligations; the fear, as Joe put it, that "professionals won't have the same values"; the potential distancing of the funder from decision making; the tendency to think that *at least* $1 million must be set aside before one can profitably make use of a foundation; the fact that having a foundation may actually create a focal point for requests rather than shield the donor from them; and the potential for children and grandchildren to alter the original intent of the donor. As Donald points out about his new foundation, there are numerous "necessary functions such as administration, research, investment counsel, safekeeping and management of the account. There are so many arrangements that [foundations can get] too wrapped up in form and too far away from their original purpose, to their detriment."

In contrast, the advantages of a foundation include the "psychic advantage of maintaining control of one's giving," as Tim puts it; the opportunity to concentrate on particular areas of interest; the chance to more carefully review proposals and evaluate outcomes; the ability to insulate oneself from fundraisers; the flexibility to respond more quickly and thoroughly to requests; and the capacity to establish legal parameters and informal training for one's children to insure that subsequent generations heed one's preferences.

A community foundation offers advantages beyond those cited above: it provides organizational resources and expertise for those just beginning to give substantial amounts; lowers the cost of administrative overhead; reduces the amount of money that must be set aside to obtain the benefits of using a foundation; allows for donor direction of grants within the broader legal and programmatic mandates of the foundation; and offers the expertise and experience of other donors within the foundation. "I appreciate what I am learning about philanthropy and try to pay back to the community," explains Steve. "But I would like to find a larger foundation with the same interests so we could pool our money and have a staff." Convenience is precisely what the Charter Fund in Denver provides, according to Gary. "Families share staff and information; checks are written by another foundation to whom we contract it out." At its best, a community foundation, says Jim, is "a university of philanthropy as well as a foundation."

It is significant that the question about organizational strategy is repeatedly phrased as "giving yourself" versus giving through a foundation. No matter what organizational strategy the wealthy advocate, the matter of "giving yourself" emerges as the underlying motif. Choosing an organizational strategy is never a trivial matter. Whether giving decisions are "closely held" or allocated to a private or community foundation, decisions about *how* to carry out philanthropy remain alongside decisions about where to contribute as an aspect of the composite identity of the wealthy donor. "Is [organizational] form an impediment to giving?" asks Carl. It's "a barrier to overcome, but you do it," replies Patrick. Despite Patrick's response, determining an organizational strategy is not just an instrumental decision but a mode of engagement. To the extent that it is "a barrier to overcome," it is a barrier to identity and not just to action. The intensity and substance of the discussion indicates that to choose a strategy of philanthropy is to choose a philanthropic identity.

Recognition versus Anonymity: Selection of Self-Identity

"Will the donor really tell the recipient what they want made public?" asks Richard, who has worked for years assisting anonymous donors in their philanthropy. "Are grantseekers told the truth? How does a recipient figure out what is the right kind and right amount of recognition to provide maximum fulfillment to the donor?" Clearly recipients may misread or violate the wishes of the donor in regard to recognition or anonymity. To prevent such mistakes, donors need to be clear about how much and what kind of recognition they desire. Thus the comments on the desirability of anonymity are, once again, not only diverse and conflicting but also revelatory of the internal conversation donors carry on concerning the appropriate approach for them to take.

Here, as on other topics, the verbal interchange among the participants seems to reflect a parallel dialogue within the individual donor. No participant was willing to stake out an absolute position on the topic of anonymity. Indeed, the tone and content of the comments seem to indicate a substantial degree of ambivalence about the right approach to take. This, I believe, is because the positive moral valence of anonymity contrasts so sharply with the fact that donors recognize, for themselves and others, the practical impact that recognition has on one's willingness to make large contributions. Anonymity, points out Richard, is really a matter of degree, adding that anonymity should be situation-specific and is best practiced only in certain instances. Ultimately, the participants go beyond simply praising anonymity or legitimating a desire for recognition. Both sides frame the issue ethically, that is, a moral case is made both for and against anonymity.[4]

The case *against* anonymity tends to revolve around how it may create an impediment to giving, undercutting what Daniel says is the potential leadership opportunity to "foster a community of giving" that occurs when donors are publicly known. Carl concurs: there "can't be a community if you're anonymous." In this view, public giving sets a model for others to follow; advances the social norm of generosity; helps identify and build a community of givers; assists donors in identifying other experienced givers whose advice and expertise may be useful; leaves open the possibility for recognition to serve as an incentive for giving; and, by providing a name along with a donation, offers recipients an additional resource for fundraising. Being identified as a donor may lead to a flood of solicitations. "But if you have a specific interest," Ted explains, "some opportunities that might not ordinarily come your way, do." His advice for reducing the intrusions associated with public giving: "Be specific about your interests."

The case *for* anonymity is equally complex and is also couched, in part, in moral language. While the case against anonymity is framed around the core value of increasing funding for a cause, the case for anonymity revolves around preserving the decision-making latitude, and advancing the moral calibre, of the donor. There are obvious—and important—instrumental advantages to protecting donors (and their children) from unwanted solicitations (being "hounded by people and organizations," as Andrew puts it), from intrusive press coverage, and from the occasional instance of harassment and threat to security. Additionally, anonymity helps donors avoid a variety of negative contingencies, such as rigidities in expectations about gift levels despite fluctuations in income (Ted); the propensity of "the press to misinterpret the giving" when "information is out of the hands of the recipient" (Ginny); and the application of pejorative stereotypes about being wealthy (Clark), especially when the gift can be viewed as self-interested, as in the case of support for a cultural institution (Mary). At the personal level, anonymity is seen as making an appeal to what Marvin calls the "right motivations," helping to guarantee virtuous giving and reducing tendencies toward ego aggrandizement. Ironically, another of its positive outcomes is precisely what those who favor recognition cite as important, namely the ability to elicit more funding for a cause. Says Clark, anonymity can be one way for a few "foreground activists" to develop a "huge pool of background people who don't want to be identified or who feel wealth has been a hassle and don't want to make it worse." There are those who "are paralyzed and do not want recognition," he explains, and so need a way to do their philanthropy "quietly" and with maximum flexibility, comfort, and ease. "People have different personalities," Beverly reminds us. "They may be shy, and such personality traits are enough to justify anonymity."

Despite the tendency to talk for or against anonymity, one participant tells me in a private conversation that he thinks it neither necessary nor appropriate to define the issue in absolute terms. He prefers the principle of *religious indifference* enunciated by Ignatius Loyola, the founder of the Jesuit religious order. He neither seeks nor avoids recognition; rather, as a result of dialogue with the recipient, he agrees to whatever tack will best accomplish the greatest spiritual and material good for all involved.

There are many other elements of the case for and against anonymity. But those mentioned by the participants during the conference are sufficient to make it clear that this most intimate aspect of philanthropy is not going to be resolved on the basis of abstract principle alone. Because the ethics of anonymity cut so keenly to the heart of one's purpose and identity as a philanthropist, the only sure thing is that donors will array strongly principled arguments in favor of both sides of the issue. It helps to be reminded by Richard that anonymity is a matter of degree and that it may be selectively practiced depending upon the circumstances of a gift. But ultimately there is more talk against than for anonymity. "There are no contributors who truly want to be anonymous—except for certain instances," insists George, while Beverly asks, "What's wrong with an ego for giving?" Indeed Marvin says, "I like the idea of being on the leadership list of a cause. Making a difference in the society *should* be a motive." Even if you are anonymous, adds Beverly, "you at least want a thank you." Moreover, remarks Mary, "A public statement about the gift and how it benefitted things would be nice," and would not violate the strictures of anonymity. Perhaps the most responsive position may be Charles's notion that the decision for or against anonymity should always be connected to some explicit evaluation of how either position contributes to achieving the greatest overall good. This position, of course, still begs the question of what the greatest good in any situation is—the topic of the next section. But whatever donors conclude about "what is to be done," their strategy invariably involves a conscientious decision about how it is to be done in regard to their own visibility. The issue of anonymity is not about the presence or absence of identity in giving, for that does not appear to be a variable. Rather, the question of anonymity is about the relative value of identifying one's self *and* about what this implies simultaneously for the effectiveness of a gift and the moral status of oneself as giver.

The Good Society and the Good Self

"So we're saying a good society is a community that cares, one that allows for private and public agencies and for human interaction," says Carl, summarizing the general consensus of the discussion about the kind of society the participants seek to enhance with their philanthropy. He goes on immediately to make the crucial connection between the social quality of such a society and the personal quality of those who shape that society. "It is one in which individuals can express their values—other-oriented rather than self-oriented ones." The good society requires the good self: "Those who are highly concerned with their own image lead to the decline of the good society." This link between the nature of the good society and the nature of the philanthropist is another instance of the unity of philanthropy and identity that emerged as the motif of the conference.

The discussion about the nature of the good society revolves around three subtopics: (1) social conditions in the United States today, (2) elements of the ideal society (which to a large extent are projections of the participants' individual activities), and (3) the role of philanthropy in transforming social conditions and creating the ideal society.

In discussing social conditions in the United States today, the philanthropists' paramount concerns are the increasing social fragmentation and attendant loss of values and sense of participation. Specific issues include multiculturalism, declining levels of public trust, low voter turnout, division between the haves and the have-nots, geographic mobility, family instability, technical specialization, lack of moral leadership, and the failures of government.

What is said about the elements of the ideal society reflects the very social fragmentation they identify as currently plaguing the country. As David remarks, "My colleagues are experts in their field but all have different absolute ideas of the good society." For Alice, "Twenty-five years of research have been spent on this question [of social welfare], yet we do not know what the new elements will be." Carl concurs: even among the best intentioned and most devoted citizens there is "no way to agree" on what exactly should become our public policies.

There are, however, two broad areas of apparent policy agreement, which show up also in the *Study on Wealth and Philanthropy*. The first is the tacit rejection of any legislative or moral imperative to radically redistribute wealth or to circumscribe the economic liberties identified with the free enterprise system. This does not mean there was no political differentiation among the participants about the types of redistribution policies deemed appropriate for bettering the lot of the nation's poor. It is just that there is a general consensus that whatever should be done to advance social welfare must be accomplished within the broad institutional framework of democratic capitalism.

The second area of consensus about the nature of the good society is a corollary of the first. It concerns the need to propagate an institutional and cultural environment of civil pluralism. The ideal society is characterized by "respect for others," says Richard, and by "an understanding of ourselves and our possible contributions." For Sam, it is easier "to turn the question around" and define a bad rather than good society. "What is justice? I don't know. But I can tell you what injustice is. I can tell you with conviction what a bad society is. I know these aren't good: state control of life and mind or spirit, lack of food and shelter, imposition of your beliefs on another." Martha agrees that the major problem is that "respect has broken down." For the downtrodden to be helped, "the fundamental prerequisite is community and good human relations." Defining the role of the individual citizen, Bill sees the single most important element as "caring for the individual," while Joe says "it is all tied to the freedom and responsibility of the individual—decentralization." The good society is self-correcting, democratic, and benevolent. It meets people's basic survival needs but goes beyond them in extending the benefits of education, health, and population control. Such a society is based on the production of wealth by a free enterprise economy, the development of good leadership, and the participation of citizens in electoral politics.

There is, finally, a broad consensus among the participants that philanthropy has an important contribution to make in creating this good society. The major role of philanthropy is to amplify "the reverse flow now taking place in society in which we're taking public policy back from Washington D.C.," maintains Carl. "We need smaller organizations, personal involvement, and a way to influence the community. The Ford Foundation and Rockefeller Foundation have served well in their time. But today we need to realize it's okay to give money away yourself. Maybe we gave these functions away [to the government] rather than the government assuming them. But the role of philanthropy is to reverse this process through small organizations that empower people."

No one argues with Harry's democratic conviction that it can be "very dangerous and expensive to have a small group setting the giving agenda for a city or region." Nevertheless, there is disagreement about the broad social strategy that should be pursued to accomplish the needed social transformation. For some, the key is to encourage individual conversion and initiative; for others it is to produce structural transformation; for still others it is to develop moral leadership. For instance, Gary says the role of philanthropy is to pay attention "to the religious and spiritual nature of human beings," while Bill asserts that philanthropy should work "to humanize people." In contrast, the role of philanthropy for Carl is to create "small organizations that empower people."

The leadership model is advocated by David, who argues that philanthropy should strive to "find the local hero who is working for change," and by Bob, who calls for philanthropists to "give money to develop leaders, direct them to a given end, and then start again with another group." Picking up on the theme of government failure, Bob insists that "we accept the wrong models. We need a community divided into small modules and get out of the idea that community is best served by the public sector. Sure we need [public sector] input but [more importantly] we need a leader." Given the fact that "our knowledge and information double in each decade, leading to specialization, more and more people know more and more about less and less," Charles explains. "A simple definition of leadership is to know what to do and how to do it," says Charles, but he acknowledges that is "more difficult" to achieve nowadays.

It is not my purpose here to evaluate or reconcile these divergent strategies. But without too much digging we unearth once again the overriding theme. However differently the participants define the good society and frame the strategies for attaining it, it is clear that a good society requires good citizens; foremost among such good citizens are good leaders, and among such good leaders are philanthropists. "A good society is not easily achieved," cautions Charles, "but working at it is better than not working at it at all." The creation of a good society includes "working at" the creation of oneself as a good philanthropist.

Philanthropy: The Next Generation

A frequent theme at the conference and in the *Study on Wealth and Philanthropy* is the relationship between parents and children surrounding the inheritance of wealth and the imparting of the parents' philanthropic concerns. It is the question, as Diane phrases it, of "How do we pass the torch?" Participants identify this theme as "passing on and passing it on." From the beginning they recognize that, from the point of view of parents and children, "passing on" means more than dying; it means the transferring of family leadership from one generation to another. Similarly, "passing it on" means more than disbursing one's wealth to others in the family; it also means the disbursement of identity and responsibility in regard to that wealth. During the conference, participants address passing on their philanthropic identity to two groups, their children and other wealthy individuals. In this context, taking giving seriously means giving others their appreciation of philanthropy. In such an effort of cultural generativity, insists Winthrop, "it is better to err on the side of more involvement rather than on the side of less."

The participants agree that passing on a philanthropic identity to their children means involving them in philanthropy early on. Whether first, second, or third generation of wealth, the participants concur that the behavior of parents is crucial for setting an example. The key, says Winthrop, is "the way they are brought up. It's by example." Marilyn, who was taught to use part of her childhood allowance for charity, says the same thing: "I think it is something you need to do by example." But, in addition to parental example, it is also important to have the children directly participate in philanthropic decisions from early in life. "If you bring [the children] into the decision-making process early, it facilitates their ability to accept their responsibility," explains Ted. Diane says the key is "instilling an education and tradition about philanthropy," for example, by "putting children in charge of certain sums of money from early on." Winthrop reports that, in his experience, an important source of philanthropic education was the practice of having "cousins' meetings in order to share information about to whom and what they give." Steve offers a similar recommendation for incorporating the next generation into the philanthropic enterprise. "Our own children come to our board meetings and we are encouraging them to serve on boards. Include your children in participating in events and they will feel part of the charity," he advises.

There is, however, something even more essential for inculcating an appreciation of philanthropy than either parental example or participation in existing family involvements. This is an effort by parents to pass on an ethical orientation toward the use of money and the social virtue of care for others. For the children of both new and old wealth who stand to inherit their parents' riches, this means learning to dispose of wealth wisely, rather than being confused and victimized by it; to develop their own priorities for giving; and to counter what Ginny admits is the occasional tendency for the "parent to be seen as 'overdoing it'—giving too much and not spending enough on oneself." Gary recognizes the validity of these objections, but stresses that educating children about philanthropy requires developing their sensitivity to the needs of others. For philanthropy to truly become a way of life for their children, parents need to "evoke some empathy in [their offspring] for some cause, such as music, the arts, the poor, and so forth."

Despite the consensus about the importance of involvement, parental example, and training, it appears that these factors are not always enough to generate a philanthropic commitment among one's children. Many participants spoke openly about how their children deviated from and sometimes even resisted their philanthropic commitment. For instance, Gary reports that his children have not yet become interested in philanthropy and, along with their friends, often "reject their parents' notions of how and to whom to give." It is part of what contributes to the perception that "the wealthy section of the baby boom generation is not generous." In the late 1960s Andrew Greeley characterized the committed, activist young adults of that time as "the new breed." It may be possible now to speak about another "new breed" of young women and men, those who have begun to receive the responsibilities and inheritances passed down from their parents. It is not the first time that the children of the wealthy have set their own course. Children of the wealthy, including the current generation of parents, have always sought to tailor any philanthropic commitment to their specific interests, which sometimes differed sharply from the designs of their parents.

Today, a complicating factor has been added to the usual new directions that mark the self-directed activity of the next generation. This is the primary commitment of children from both established and entrepreneurial wealth to make their own mark in the world of business, investment, the arts, and the professions. Increasingly, it appears that many daughters and sons of the wealthy want first to establish an active economic life *before* entering the distributive realms of philanthropy. "I grew up in a wealthy family where I was not expected to work," says Martha. "But internally I needed to work and so headed an alternative school for six years." The identity these individuals are building does not exclude philanthropy, but it is one surrounding the active creation of their identity first in spheres in which they are themselves actively generative rather than distributive.

For some, the project of public self-expression takes the form of philanthropy—conventional or innovative. Clearly, the philanthropic projects described by many of the conference participants are highly innovative and entrepreneurial. They represent hands-on efforts by the wealthy donors themselves to apply new ideas and approaches to issues of social concern. Indeed, a number of the participants are themselves relatively young men and women who have used their inheritances to establish new organizational and substantive directions in philanthropy. For instance, Clark explained how he and other young inheritors established community foundations, such as the Vanguard Foundation, in order to fulfill the "common desire to give money away in their own way." For his generation, "the problem has not been whether or not to give, but how to give," since, as he remarks, his "family has wealth in great excess." This does not mean that everyone from his generation takes the same approach. His sister, for example, "doesn't give much money but does give time." Still, the comments of those parents in attendance point to what may be a new reluctance by their children to replicate immediately their parents' philanthropic identity. The children of entrepreneurs want the chance to make the kind of independent economic or professional mark their parents made. At the same time, the children of established wealthy families also seek to make an independent mark, not just by changing the direction of family philanthropy (as was often the case for the generation preceding them), but by striking out on their own in business, investment, and the professions. Ginny's observation that "giving is something that people tend to do at an older age" is not an entirely accurate impression. There has always been substantial philanthropic involvement by the wealthy even while they were relatively young, as the presence of Clark and other young donors at the conference attests. But this may be changing as today's generation of inheritors seeks first to find its productive place in the world. Deborah, for example, points out that, now that the family wealth has passed to the third generation, a new tension has arisen as her children manifest a greater concern for business than philanthropy. Not only is it the case that the "younger generation has less money," she explains, but that the money itself "is less personal." As a result, the children tend to go along with existing foundation activity but are not actively involved themselves at this point.

One crucial new piece of information generated by the conference, then, may be that young wealthy individuals may not be, early on, as active in philanthropy as their parents or the previous generation of young inheritors may desire. It is not of course possible to "prove" from the anecdotal conference data the trend of young inheritors toward professional careers and away from early philanthropic involvement. Nor does this mean that the new inheritors will remain disengaged from philanthropy forever. It could simply mean that philanthropy is being put off, so to speak, to "an older age"—not simply in the sense of chronological age but professional age. Perhaps the sequencing of career and philanthropy carried out by such business luminaries as Geoffrey T. Boisi and Peter S. Lynch will be the more common model of the rising generation of the wealthy. Both Boisi, formerly the number three executive at Goldman Sachs, and Lynch, the former manager of Fidelity's brilliantly performing Magellan Fund, stepped down from their positions at the zenith of their careers in order to devote their efforts to family and philanthropy.

Go and Do Likewise: Inculcating a Philanthropic Identity in Other Wealthy Individuals

The discussion about passing on a philanthropic identity to other wealthy people focused primarily on those who were not brought up with at least some implicit orientation toward giving. With the exception of the most recent generation, who may be more inclined to delay philanthropic involvement for the reasons reviewed in the previous section, those who have inherited wealth have tended to inherit an orientation toward philanthropy along with their financial inheritance. From early on, these heirs are imbued with a tripartite understanding of their wealth.[5] Wealth is divided first between principal or capital, on one side, and interest on the other. In turn, the latter is divided between consumption under the rubric of living expenses and distribution under the rubric of philanthropy. In this model, philanthropy is part and parcel of an identity and strategy of wealth. A category of money is set aside for giving such that participating in philanthropy is not problematic. At the same time, however, the very orientation that sets aside money for philanthropy also tends to restrict its amount. Philanthropy is characteristically part of one's social responsibility as a wealthy individual, but because philanthropy is to be conducted out of the earnings on capital, it remains quantitatively limited. Now, many who have inherited wealth, including many of those participating in the conference, do "violate" this unwritten law of limited philanthropy, curtailing living expenses and spending down their capital. For the wealthy from established families, then, participation in philanthropy is less about creating *de novo* a philanthropic involvement than about expanding their commitment.

In contrast, for entrepreneurs (and their entrepreneurial children) the task is different. Where there is no personal or family history of philanthropy, one must be created. This is never simple or automatic. Of all the wealthy, entrepreneurs are the most likely to be busily engaged in day-to-day business operations and, until they begin to obtain a substantial cash flow from their asset-rich but non-liquid investments, they are the least likely to have a large reserve of disposable income that can be dedicated to philanthropy. Still, as with those who have inherited wealth, there is no rigid pattern to which every entrepreneur adheres. The *Study on Wealth and Philanthropy* confirms what was indicated by the conference participants, that some entrepreneurs engage in philanthropy from the outset of their business careers, and engage generously. But if a major obstacle to taking giving seriously among those who have inherited wealth is the conception of capital as "untouchable," a major obstacle for entrepreneurs is non-liquidity.

The important point to keep in mind is that different strategies are required for getting members of established wealthy families and entrepreneurs to take giving seriously. For the former, the question tends to be encouraging the intensity of commitment rather than creating an initial philanthropic orientation. For the latter, the task tends to be creating an initial orientation. But once that is accomplished, generous giving may flow more automatically, since they lack the preservation instinct regarding a family capital trust bequeathed to their stewardship. Thus, for both those who have inherited their wealth and those who have earned it, there is need for philanthropic socialization—that is, bringing into their purview the challenge of growth in philanthropic identity that those at the conference have themselves undergone.

Acquiring a Philanthropic Identity

The previous sections summarizing the conference discussions have found in these discussions an underlying motif of philanthropy as identity formation. The conference discussions that were specifically on this topic provide an abbreviated (compared to the *Study on Wealth and Philanthropy*) but consistent view about how the wealthy actually come to obtain a philanthropic identity. Because the process of forming a philanthropic identity is key to understanding how wealthy individuals come to take giving seriously, I will take time, first, to summarize what was voiced by the conference participants, and then to elaborate a fuller model of identity formation as exemplified by participants in the study. In both sections, we accept Daniel's position that the goal is that "you have to have that basic notion to give," and, hence the key questions are "How do you make giving a part of everyone's lives? How do you convince people to give?" How, in Fred's words, is it possible to help others realize the maxim, "giving [is] the greatest thing about living."

Socialization to a philanthropic identity includes experiences that lead to a more mature sense of responsibility and to community, which instills the expectation of such responsibility. Presumably, Sam is speaking autobiographically when he explains that "maturity comes [to the wealthy] when they realize there is no answer to the randomness of human experience. Being hung up on that is pointless. The question must shift from 'Why [are you wealthy and others are not]?' to 'What do you do with it?'" The opportunity for anonymity may be helpful at the outset, because prospective philanthropists may feel "hassled" or "paralyzed" by their wealth, Sam says. But equally important may be the incorporation of the uncommitted into a community explicitly created for them, such as the Vanguard Foundation, to overcome their isolation. What Sam suggests for others directly parallels the process of identity formation that the wealthy at the conference have themselves experienced.

In previous research I have located six related factors that lead to a philanthropic identity, all of which, in one way or another, the participants also stressed during the course of the conference. The first mobilizing factor is a *community of participation*—an organizational setting in which philanthropy is expected or at least invited by the fact of being active in the organization. As John says, "My giving is to causes I'm most involved in and most interested in." "There was no influence, parents or others, who taught me the value of giving," he explains, so "my philanthropy comes solely from involvement in various projects." Doug expresses the same thing with the simple formula that "Involvement precedes giving." "The more exposure there is to the ideas in the community," says Sharon, "the more people will become interested in giving to things." Specifically, we see the wealthy introduced to philanthropy through family, work, and voluntary activities. "My father died early and I wound up as the family member in charge of continuing his directions," recalls Earl, "so I took it for granted that philanthropy would be part of my responsibilities." For Tim the introduction to philanthropy began when he became a board member and later part-time president of a foundation. Strange as it may seem, the tax structure also serves as a pseudo-community influencing philanthropic involvement. "Wanting to avoid giving half of your estate away to the tax man is a primary motivation," John explains, so "future estate planning is a must."

The second mobilizing factor is a *framework of consciousness* that makes philanthropy a priority. Here, religion, guilt, and politics are mentioned by the participants. Recalling his visit to the Sistine Chapel two years ago, Charles explains how the mural of the Last Judgment, in which the sheep are separated from the goats, relates to his motivation. For him, the "bottom line of philanthropy is trying to get myself there among the sheep and help others get there." In the case of Sam, philanthropy is "a way of dealing with guilt over receiving money, which is a strain." "Why did I get all this money as opposed to my best friend Neil, who didn't get a thing and works in a factory?" he asks. According to Clark, philanthropy is one element of a therapy for the rich, to deal with their guilt about being wealthy. "If the kids *don't* feel guilty, they may not feel the need to give." The motivation behind Martha's involvements is that of a politics focused on the empowerment of the oppressed. She dropped her family name at the age of 21 and "went to Rio and lived with squatters." As a result of this experience she learned the "profound revelation which helped the rest of my life," namely that philanthropy is "not only an activity of giving away, but also of sharing."

A third factor, mentioned by Fred, is something that many wealthy philanthropists reported in the *Study on Wealth and Philanthropy.* This is the effect of an *early childhood experience* in which a parent or other admired adult teaches the importance of charity by word or example. For instance, when Fred "started washing windows at age nine," his mother told him to "give away ten percent" of his earnings. We might recall here what was noted earlier about the importance of parental example: the need, as Ted put it, to "bring [the children] into the decision making process early"; and the desirability, according to Diane, of "putting children in charge of certain sums of money from early on."

A fourth important factor is interaction with a *socializing agent*, a person or organization that in some way provides an introductory path into the moral and institutional responsibilities of philanthropy. Parents and other childhood models, as I noted, serve in this capacity earlier in life. But for those who lack such models or have failed to follow in their footsteps, adult encounters with such agents are crucial for establishing a philanthropic identity. Fred recounts that he and his wife were introduced to philanthropy as a result of benefiting from someone else's largesse. "My wife came from a family with no money. A doctor offered her an interest-free loan when she got pregnant and stopped working. He later wrote to say his gift to the baby was forgiving the loan. He told us to pass it on, and we did it immediately. We passed it on through anonymous gifts to a college, and whenever it becomes possible, we do it for someone else." The Jewish community, as will be exemplified below, is well known for directly prodding financially well-off Jews into an initial, and subsequently intensified, philanthropic commitment. This notion of the importance of the socializing agent is also a consistent finding of survey research on philanthropy. "Being asked," especially by someone who is known and respected by the potential donor, is a major determinant of giving. "It is difficult for professionals to approach the wealthy," remarks Clark; "it is easier among peers to encourage each other to give more and also in better ways." According to Diane, the "peer-to-peer relationship is what makes it work." Thus Gary is quite correct that it is "by example and not by intellectual discussions" that much philanthropy is generated. For his part, George tries to "spend time in an exchange of ideas with individuals of means who have been creative in their giving—those who are proactive." From the point of view of someone who has served as a socializing agent in conjunction with his various board positions, Daniel remarks that "you almost want people to feel embarrassed because they don't give." Charles suggests an alternative, positive tactic for socializing agents: "Find out what [potential donors] want," he says, and help them see how "philanthropy might be the vehicle" to accomplish their goals.

In addition, there are important socializing experiences that occur as a result of personal contact with those in need in a foreign environment. For Martha it was "going overseas to live in Brazil and do social work in squatter settlements." As she explains, "It's important to think about what you bring back to your own culture. The contrast with how differently people live with different resources is etched on my consciousness. It never fades. It's compelling. It changes one's lifestyle and goal in giving, which for me is global. Such intercultural experience helped put things in perspective." Similarly, Fred explains how he has both "taken and helped lead Third World trips," for instance to India, where he worked with Mother Teresa's community. Like Martha, the upshot of his experience was an increase in his philanthropic commitment, especially around forging the link between first-world wealth and third- world poverty. But, in contrast to Martha, his experience led him to focus more on the "impoverishment of spirit, the lack of access to others, and the absence of feeling a part of community" that plague the soul of many North Americans. As his time in Calcutta came to an end, Fred informed Mother Teresa that he was thinking of retiring in order to serve with her group in India. But Mother Teresa encouraged a different tack. "She said that nowhere was there as much loneliness as in affluent America. 'Go back where God put you, to live simply but well,' she said."

A fifth mobilizing factor is that those who set out on a philanthropic path experience a broad array of *reinforcing intrinsic rewards*. Philanthropy becomes its own reward and encourages deeper commitment. "What appeals to me is to be creative in helping solve a problem," says George. According to Martha, philanthropy provides "a way for her to be a human bridge as well as a supporter of organizations and supporter of the bonds we see in communities that work." Philanthropy is her way "of developing [her] spirit and having access to others." There are, of course, negative experiences that can deter one from more substantial philanthropic involvement. Gary points out that there can be a "loss of credibility for a whole philanthropic area that happens [when someone undergoes] an unreliable philanthropic experience." The unfortunate consequence of such a circumstance, he explains, is that it "lowers self-esteem and makes the individual angry at [charitable] institutions."

Taken together, these five factors, along with a sixth—the subjective realization that one has liquid resources to devote to philanthropy—result in a more or less intense *philanthropic identity*. The participants had much to say about this, although most of it was interspersed with their comments on other subjects. In the next section I address the connection between taking giving seriously and the existence of a moral identity in which identification with others is the key element. As we listen to comments of the conference participants, however, it is possible to find more than a little appreciation of the ideal elements of a charitable vocation. Such a vocation, we learn, is ultimately a moral dedication not so much to be selfless, as is often thought, but to engage the self in a more profound way. "The key" to a philanthropic identity, emphasizes Charles, "is having a mission, some goals you wish to accomplish." Sam depicts the search for a deeper identity as a spiritual pilgrimage revolving around the biblical adage that "to find yourself you have to lose yourself.

It's one's own responsibility to take the journey. It's a personal journey and one that must come to answers."

Moving to a philanthropic identity is essentially a matter of personal transformation. "Giving is so important because it helps us to become other-oriented," explains Fred. Something spiritual happens to the wealthy donor that is comparable to what the donor seeks to accomplish by way of social effect. Taking giving seriously involves what Jesuit theologian Karl Rahner calls a transposition from "having to" to "wanting to." Says Clark, "Once you feel in your heart that you morally must give, then you want to give." In his case, "the ability to not *have* to work" [my emphasis] opens the opportunity "to contribute fulltime." Martha expresses the positive reversal in orientation as the "personal, spiritual journey [entailed in] shifting from feeling guilty." "Each of us needs to find that bridge" over isolation and separation, she explains, "as we work to do our philanthropy."

NARRATIVE OF MORAL IDENTITY

In the foregoing analysis I have attempted to make the case that taking giving seriously entails the construction of a certain kind of moral identity. Such a moral identity does not characterize the self-consciousness of all wealthy philanthropists, even all of the most generous ones. Nor is such a moral identity the preserve of the wealthy; a similar intensity of dedication to the care of others is evinced by good-hearted individuals from all economic strata. But because my purpose in this essay is to explore the nature of a committed philanthropic identity as it occurs among the wealthy and because the statements I have drawn upon for my analysis were necessarily disjointed, due to the conference format, I believe it will be instructive to see how the identity-formation process is revealed in a more extended narrative format. For this more systematic analysis, I draw upon an interview from the *Study on Wealth and Philanthropy.*

To review, the six elements of the identity-formation process of a serious wealthy philanthropist are (1) a community of participation, (2) a framework of consciousness, (3) a childhood experience, (4) adult interaction with socializing agents, (5) positively reinforcing philanthropic involvements, and (6) recognition of disposable resources. These six mobilizing factors are seldom, if ever, equally influential in the life of a particular individual. However, the narrative of Benjamin Ellman, a Jewish entrepreneur, clearly exhibits four of the mobilizing factors and refers to the remaining two in passing.

Benjamin Ellman is a 56-year-old native of Chicago whose father owned a chain of dime stores. Most of his wealth, however, he made on his own through his hotel supply business. The following excerpts from the transcript of his interview document the role of four mobilizing factors: a community of participation, a framework of consciousness, socializing agents, and reinforcing experiences. In addition, Ellman alludes to how his philanthropy was set in motion only when his business attained a certain level of success, and he speaks about the absence of childhood models for philanthropy.

> My first roles in philanthropy or in civic activities came through the Jewish community, when I was still starting to become fairly successful in life. . . . I was exposed by people from [the Jewish Community], elder people who I had a lot of respect for *[community of participation.]*. People who had built businesses, who were nice people who had helped me out. And they brought me into some of these [philanthropic activities] and exposed me to the needs. And I felt that it was important that as you do better, that you give something back *[socializing agents]*. . . .
>
> They were kind of—they took on a role, too. My parents died quite young. When I started becoming more successful and affluent *[disposable resources]*, instead of, you know, talking about things with your father and mother, as you would normally, I would be talking about those kinds of things with other people *[initiatory childhood experience]*. So some of these other people who I admired a lot were very interested in Jewish community activities and they got me involved. And I saw the needs in it. It just seemed important that somebody had helped my antecedents when they came to

this country many years ago and that I should probably do the same thing *[framework of consciousness]*. So that's how I first got involved in giving some monies, let's say, to Jewish activities. And then, they would ask me to participate. And I went through a young leadership group that they were putting together in those days—the Jewish Federation here in Chicago *[socializing agents]*. And I became rather interested in things like welfare. Care of the mentally retarded. Care of older people. Problems of broken homes. I got the knowledge of that, which I had never known about. And it interested me. And I then became very much involved. Then, because of that and because I am a leadership-type person, I became presidents of things *[reinforcing community of participation]*. I came on boards of directors and I became presidents. And from then—I went from that—I would go into the general community, to where I'm involved today in other things that aren't necessarily particularly Jewish. . . .

[Q: Why haven't you decided to devote all your time to philanthropy?]

Well, because that hasn't interested me. I mean, I don't know what I would do. I'd be bored to death, probably. I mean, I'm not ready to disinvest myself from business —to walk away. . . . And why do I [also involve myself in philanthropy]? I do it because it's interesting. I think that you, you get involved with things that are different from things that you do in a business way of life and that's good because it makes you a more well-rounded person. So I get, you know, when I get involved in the university or community center, or a hospital or something like that—that's giving me something back, not just in a philanthropic or a social welfare way, but it's almost like an interest other than what I do on a daily business basis, which is important. It makes me more well-rounded. . . . So, so when I get involved in other areas, it just widens my scope of interest and expands my mind. And I enjoy it. So I think that's a lot of the reasons I do those things today *[reinforcing framework of consciousness]*. . . .

> I think basically when people give, they give for themselves. I think that they get more out of it down the line than what they think they'll get out of it. I'm not talking about the normal gifts you have to make in the form of business where you give to this because this guy gets you to give to this—that kind of stuff where you're simply [dealing with] suppliers and that sort of thing. I'm talking about major gifts. . . . Giving has nothing to do with status. I really don't think you get status from giving. But I think you get satisfaction. That's very good, you know. I just really think that giving is a part of getting. I think you get back a lot, too. First of all, obviously, you feel satisfied because you've done something. Secondly, in many instances where you've done things, you can actually see the concrete results for people, huge things in their lives *[reinforcing framework of consciousness]*.

Not every life story of a wealthy philanthropist so explicitly demonstrates the six elements leading to a moral identity of charity. But, drawing on Benjamin Ellman's narrative, we are able to see in one biography the identity-formation process we pieced together from the abbreviated interactions of the conference participants. Apparently Ellman, like the conference sponsors, recognizes an important difference between participation in philanthropy as a peripheral or derivative formality and as a serious moral identity. Such an identity does not emerge full-blown from the head of Zeus. Rather, it results from a process of learning in which other agents initiate the potential philanthropist into a deeper sense of charitable responsibility, practice, and self-consciousness. In addition, once a serious beginning has been made, it is important that positive extrinsic and intrinsic rewards reinforce and intensify the philanthropic vocation.

Notes

1. All conference participants are identified by pseudonyms to preserve confidentiality.

2. For a detailed discussion of the methodology, sampling, and findings, see Schervish and Andrew Herman (1988).

3. Since the sessions were not recorded, I do not have the verbatim statements made by participants. But it is possible to capture the main thrust of the discussion from the handwritten notes provided by the scribes assigned to the various sessions. Throughout the paper I have quoted these notes, attributing them (by means of pseudonyms) to the particular participant whose comments the notes summarized. In some instances these notes represent verbatim statements made by the participants. But in most cases the notes—and my quotations—in fact paraphrase the participants' comments.

4. For a more extensive discussion of the case for and against anonymity, see Schervish (1990).

5. See Schervish and Herman (1988) especially Chapters 4 and 5 on the biographical patterns of those who have inherited wealth and the section on noblesse oblige philanthropy in Chapter 6.

RICH IS BEAUTIFUL

Obie Benz

This chapter was written under a pseudonym by Obie Benz and was published by the Co-Evolution Quarterly in 1974. Mr. Benz had inherited money at age 21 and, having already supported social change causes as an organizer, felt compelled to learn how to contribute philanthropically as well. In 1971 he founded the Vanguard Foundation, where donors pooled funds for collective grantmaking in the San Francisco Bay area.

Mr. Benz also organized conferences to help inheritors make good philanthropic decisions and learn how to address the personal side of their wealth. The network of organizations that these meetings helped spawn, the Funding Exchange, now makes grants of over $7 million a year from 14 offices throughout the country.

The title of the article was an ironic take-off from the 60's "black is beautiful" slogan—and was intended to help young people with inherited money to address the special conflicts created by being different from their peers in that one important way. In the spirit of "self-help" the article discusses problems confronting inheritors: what percentage of income to give, which causes to support and in what proportions, what degree of anonymity to maintain, etc.

The article has two parts: an analysis of the condition of having both inherited money and a social conscience, and the minutes of a meeting of a group of 15 people. The material in both parts has been either excerpted or paraphrased, reducing the article to half its original length.

A good case can be made that the children of wealthy families are brought up in deprived situations. Many of them lived in households where their parents were frequently absent, where they were brought up by servants and did not have the advantages of a consistent role model with whom to identify. Many were brought up in large households with plenty of objects but few friends and close contacts, and were forced to sit through endless, stiff dinners at large tables where they couldn't play with their food. Most did not come into contact with the whole range of classes in our society. One friend of mine was driven to school every day in a chauffeur-driven limousine and hated it, feeling lonely and wishing he could take the bus like everyone else.

When I was growing up, I suddenly realized that there were actually people who didn't live in big houses and go away on vacations all the time. I started to see a widening discrepancy between the way I lived and the way a lot of other people lived. It didn't seem fair. But what could I do? My parents were my parents, and I lived the life they provided for me.

Times changed a lot during the sixties, and many people developed a heightened sense of social responsibility. By studying social theory and volunteering for work in low-income communities, I began to understand that, directly or indirectly, the wealthy class was to some degree responsible for oppression on the basis of race and sex, for United States aggression and destruction abroad, and for the maintenance of our vastly inequitable system. Our industries, controlled entirely by the wealthy, seemed bent on destroying much of the world's natural beauty and making life impossible for various species of plants and animals, including, potentially, our own.

Exploitation by the wealthy came up again and again—in conversations about the French revolution, in articles about corporate resistance to pollution controls, at anti-war rallies, and in the classroom. Wherever I went, I was constantly battered by the idea that people like me were ripping off the rest of the world. Now, of course, I knew that I wasn't ripping off the world—but somebody was, and it wasn't the poor people. This became incredibly confusing: I knew that my parents and their friends were generally good, moral, honest people, but I realized that there was some truth to these generalizations and class analyses.

Then, when I became twenty-one, I came into a trust fund with a lot of money in it. Nobody asked me; I didn't have to do anything. All of a sudden, one day there it was. I was rich myself!

I discovered that, when you have a lot of money, you start getting an income of about five percent each year, no matter what you do. So I started getting an income far above what I could spend, even if I wanted to be extravagant. What was I going to do with all that money? There were only a few alternatives: I could reinvest it, give it away, or buy things. But the choice had to be made.

At first I felt a great elation: "Wow, I can do just about anything I want—travel, buy camera equipment—I'm not going to have to work for a living!" I could set up a newspaper or start a company. All I had to do was decide among my options.

But it became apparent very quickly that an abundance of options was not necessarily good, as there seemed to be a subtle trap built into most of them. If I depended heavily on money to do something, such as buy and set up a farm, there was a real danger of using the money to avoid grappling with the kinds of problems that face every other farmer, problems which would teach me the real roots of the trade. Of course, I could probably learn these roots other ways, but how would I know how much of the accomplishment was me and how much the money?

Then came a whole series of complicated personal questions involving friends, which I had never imagined before. How could I buy a farm and do just what I wanted, when my best friend and his wife had to work part-time just to earn enough to eat and pay the rent while going through school? Simple. I could just give them enough money so that they wouldn't have to work either! But then, how would I choose which of my working friends to patronize, and what would happen to my relationship with the people I was giving $100 a week? And what would happen to my relationship with everyone else when the word started to get around?

Luckily, as my friends and I were close, I was able to talk about my feeling with them (they said they couldn't imagine taking money from me). But I became incredibly hung up and guilty about the fact that it wasn't fair for me to have all this money while other people didn't. I felt as if I wanted to give some to just about everyone, but knew that I couldn't. I wanted to give to social causes, but it was so complicated to choose which ones that I didn't know where to start. So I just decided to let things ride and left the responsibility of deciding to the family broker, who, predictably, decided the money should be invested: a cop-out for me, in a sense, but just as much a step towards self-preservation.

Many young people with money develop a passion for secrecy, having hated the way they were treated during their childhoods when people found out they were from rich families. Recognition often brought a new dimension to the relationship: curiosity, suspicion, attraction, dislike, or a weird kind of respect, a deference. At times the reaction was powerful, but, in any case, it had little to do with who they really were.

Having an identifiable name is another giant step beyond just being rich. Once a friend of mine was at a party and introduced herself to a person who wouldn't give her the time of day. When the person found out who her father was, she couldn't get rid of him. When a girl from a particularly well-known family was eleven years old and at summer camp, she was asked by another camper for her autograph. This same friend said, "Once I was in a medical clinic waiting room and, after I gave my name to the nurse, one of the other patients seriously asked me if she could touch me."

I went through a long stage when only my very best friends knew I had inherited money. I didn't buy a record player or anything that would imply wealth, avoided talking about and even lied about vacations I had taken, became overbearingly bargain-conscious, and always dressed in the most neutral clothes possible. Several people I know have moved from the East Coast to the West Coast, or vice versa, to avoid surroundings where other people knew of their family backgrounds. One woman changed her name (fears of a Patty Hearst-style kidnapping played a part here as well). Another worked full-time as a maid for seventy dollars a week.

And there was also the pervasive fear that people were going to ask for money. I was afraid that, if people knew I was rich, they would think: "Now I need $200 to pay the rent or I'm going to get thrown out, and that is an incredible amount of money for me. That person over there is rich, could write out a check for $200 without blinking, and would never miss it." Of course they would be right as far as the money was concerned. The $200 would make very little difference.

But the sacrifice would not be monetary. Since money is purely numerical, it's easy to get tricked into thinking that there is nothing more to it than the numbers on the bills and how many bills there are. Lending and receiving money creates a bond, like giving someone a job, and there is a certain sense in which the lender is the boss. While this can be acceptable and workable, a relationship with "boss" overtones can have some very uncomfortable, unequal vibrations, which make a positive, open relationship much more difficult. On the rare occasions when I have lent money, often the most uncomfortable part has been our trying too hard to ignore these vibrations, which is just as deadening.

Beyond the personal difficulties, a further fear was that people would feel I ought to lend them money even though they weren't as close friends as lending protocol usually requires. This could lead to a ridiculous deluge of requests. In any case, whether or not people were actually going to ask for money, I was terrified of the idea that I would have to suspect people's motives if they were especially friendly. Is this person really interested in me or is she just after my money? What would it be like to have to ask this question every time I met someone who might know I had money? At the time, it seemed much easier to hide the fact that I was rich.

Another problem for wealthy people is whether or not to work for pay. A lot of people think (and have said) that, no matter where you work, you are ripping other people off if you have a steady income but take a salary anyway. When I applied for jobs that had several applicants I felt guilty, thinking that, if I won, I would be denying someone a livelihood. I didn't need the money, so why not work for free? But this gets into the same kind of confidence problems as the issue of personal relations. Assuming I chose to work for free, would they still want me to work there if they had to pay me the same as everyone else? The "pay on the basis of need" idea can ignore the fact that a salary means more than just cash.

Being rich is like being an extraordinarily beautiful woman. It is something that almost everyone notices, and most are attracted to. Other women wish they were like you; men wish they had you. The people you don't want to come on to you do, and ones you do want to come on to you don't. You get thrown into more situations than most people and have to expend that much more energy dealing with them all. You are in danger of getting sidetracked by people or situations that aren't right for you. People tend to notice that one striking part of you, ignoring your real skills and the things that are important to you. People somehow expect more from you and are quicker to judge. They compare themselves to you and get competitive, no matter how you relate to them. You fit into a social stereotype that is supposed to be eminently desirable and remind people of all their own past feelings about their inability to achieve that stereotype. People assume that you must be happy and satisfied and that things come easily to you.

But, most of all, you are in danger of liking yourself for that quality which, in reality, is without substance and satisfies only a fragment of your needs. Placing much stock in this particular "quality" can lead to wasting an immense amount of time and missing many good opportunities that you may or may not ever know you missed.

Some of the most beautiful women are also the most unhappy and have the least idea how to improve their lives. Their most noticeable and obvious quality, their looks, is the very thing that holds them back. While confused and lonely, they can go along relying on their beauty, deceived into thinking they're on top. Possessing wealth, like beauty, has no meritorious or substantial qualities, and pitfalls lurk at every turn. The ability to purchase objects and live without working can leave you at forty in a big, boring house with nothing to do. You're not born with a silver spoon that helps you cope with reality.

No matter how hard I tried to ignore it, I was plagued by having this extra money around and not using it for the causes I believed in. It seemed to me that if people have a social responsibility to contribute to the common good, and if they have some moral responsibility to utilize their potential, then they had to give money away, if they had it to give. To ignore the money seemed to be as much a positive decision as giving it away; I felt just as responsible for what I didn't do as for what I did do.

In other words, if you walk by a pond, find someone drowning, throw him a rope, and pull him out, you have saved his life and are responsible for saving his life. If you walk by, find a person drowning, see the rope, notice the patterns of the ripples from his thrashing, and keep on walking, you have let the person drown and are as responsible for his death as if you shot him in the head.

When we are facing a multitude of potentially disastrous situations—fluorocarbons in the atmosphere, worldwide famine, international terrorism and blackmail, the disintegration of the international money system, the deterioration of the environment—we cannot just sit and watch. Many people are acting as if we were still in the mid-1920s. Our society slavers after the more-and-more-and-more lifestyle with such abandon that few even consider how it all ties together. It's like a man in the driver's seat of his car, his foot jamming the accelerator to the floor, staring mesmerized into the ascending speedometer with an occasional satisfied glance in the rearview mirror.

Money is an important factor in the evolution of most groups doing constructive work in our society. There are also billions being spent by the other side: by corporations interested in profit at the expense of safety and the environment, by governments preoccupied with world domination at the expense of social programs, by bureaucracies more concerned with their own perpetuation than with the public welfare, by wealthy people more concerned with making greater profits than with anything else.

There are so few people seriously concerned with social and environmental problems that those of us who are, and have the financial resources to help, can't afford to sit and watch some group like the Atomic Energy Commission tell us, "We'll figure out what to do with that extra plutonium sometime; the point is that we need more energy now to sustain our economy." The United States might not need so much energy if it started moving toward a no-growth economy and started using less than thirty-three percent of the world's resources for its five percent of the world's population. There are endless projects focusing on the rights of individuals, equality between people, the power of people to be involved in decisions that directly affect them, the preservation of our natural environment, etc., etc. All of them need money desperately.

But I don't want to give the "if you're not with us, you're against us" impression. It is difficult to give money away well, and there will inevitably be a long learning process. A little money can go a very long way when it is applied carefully and at the right time. Of course, it can also be wasted or actually be destructive if it is applied at the wrong place or at the wrong time.

Incredibly complex factors have to be considered and balanced against each other. Do you fund a free breakfast program for ghetto children, or a group trying to get the city government to pay for it? Do you fund a lawsuit to outlaw isolation cells, or a film on prison reform to be used as an educational tool? Do you fund the National Free Clinic Council where your contribution will be a small percentage of their total budget, or a local clinic where your contribution will be half of what they need? Do you fund an experimental group doing research into solar energy or an organization fighting increases in utility bills? Do you fund Ralph Nader, or the Environmental Defense Fund, or a tenants' union, or the United Farm Workers, or a women's employment group? Or do you cash it all in for several truckloads of spare change and head for 42nd Street?

Money is raw energy, like a flame. In order to be used effectively, it has to be carefully directed. It should certainly not be used carelessly or haphazardly, though it invites such use. The discovery of fire led to the immediate discovery of a whole set of rules that had to be respected or you burned down your grass hut.

While many problems stem directly from the mechanical considerations intrinsic to using money as a tool, there are strong, personal side-effects, which are not necessarily obvious. Intuition is not always sufficient to deal with the sticky situations created by these emotional factors.

As alluded to before, my first reaction was to fund people who were friends. However, not only would this ignore the question of what would be most effective, but the "boss" overtones would be very difficult to fight. For instance, if I funded someone for a year or two, how would I decide to stop and move to something else, especially if the person would not be able to find money elsewhere to do the same thing? Who wants to be put in the position of evaluating the performance of friends? Several people I've met refuse to give money to friends under any circumstances, citing histories of good friendships that were unpredictably broken because of money hassles.

Whether with friends or not, just talking to someone about giving them money carries a commitment, and this relationship has to be dealt with sensitively on both sides. The giver has to be careful not to let his objective evaluation be clouded too much by factors like his own guilt, pressures from other people, or the extent of need of the people asking (a fantastic number of people have great need—do you feed one hungry person or buy seeds for two?). The person asking has to be careful to stay honest and not let distaste for the "supplicant" role get too personal.

Evaluating applicants is an acquired skill. I became incredibly drained while floundering around in the beginning. A good number of the people I turned down got angry and hostile and made sure I understood how they felt. Many donors try to separate themselves emotionally from people they are funding until they feel comfortable with their role (if ever).

Some people have hired a director who assumes the responsibility of dealing with applicants and interviews. They remain on the decision-making board, along with the director, to make final decisions on specific groups, basing their views largely on the director's report. One person I know considers it to be a great relief that she doesn't have to talk directly with applicants, which she had done for a long time, because that was getting very uncomfortable. Another keeps personally in touch with some of the groups funded, while letting the director do most of the busy work. This enables him to keep a distance from the mechanics while benefiting from direct contact, which helps him learn how to evaluate applicants and assess their effectiveness.

Other people have set up foundations with a director and a decision-making board made up of people they trust. They then have no more to do with it, except to check in once or twice a year to see how things are going. This kind of foundation can either be set up to fund within certain guidelines or be left to the discretion of the board. The Third World Control Fund of San Francisco, where all decisions are made by third world people, is an example of the latter.

A foundation should never spend more than ten percent on the process of giving money, and much less, or nothing, is desirable. So it's hard to hire someone and set up an office unless there is more than $100,000 a year to give away. If someone has less than that to give but still wants to have some entity for applicants to contact, he can join or start a collective donor group.

One such group is the Vanguard Foundation, of which I am a member, where fifteen people pool a portion of their annual incomes to give away. We do the administrative work ourselves (two full-time people without pay), interview applicants personally (anywhere from two to ten foundation members show up), and make decisions by consensus at meetings every three weeks. We fund small, social change projects in the San Francisco Bay area that don't have access to other funding. All of our grantees must be nonprofit; our main priorities are prison reform, women's rights, third world groups, alternative media, consumer groups, and economic alternatives. We've been going now for three years and give away about $90,000 a year. Grants are usually in the $1,000 to $2,000 range.

Another kind of donor group is the Haymarket Foundation in Boston. Haymarket was originally modeled after Vanguard but is evolving to be more of an alternative community chest. Decisions are made not by a collective donor process, but by a board of community activists and by the donors as individuals. While much of their initial funding came from wealthy young people, they are developing a broad base of support from people of all economic strata. There is a service within the foundation for people who want administrative help and advice about giving money. Haymarket has funding priorities similar to those of Vanguard, though it concentrates on community organization as a means to redistribute power to low-income and other minority groups. While Haymarket emphasizes the Boston area, it does fund in other New England areas when activist groups in those areas have no other access to funds.

There is another group of sixteen people from different parts of the country who meet once every three or four months to exchange ideas and discuss specific problems related to their backgrounds, inheriting wealth, and giving money away. Minutes of one of those meetings are printed along with this article.

Several people started this group because we felt a need to talk with others but did not have a Haymarket or a Vanguard to turn to. In spite of the fact that none of us had known each other before, we decided to get together once to see what would happen. We were surprised to find we had a great deal to share and felt the meeting was incredibly rewarding. We are now trying to figure out how to expand this group so that it can include more people, without limiting the good group interaction we've been able to develop because of our relatively small numbers.

So much for different ways to deal with giving money. Let me just mention one good question that people ask all the time: "If you're so concerned with the inequities of the system, why not give away all your money?" First, many people I've met have been given irrevocable trusts that cannot be broken under any circumstances; all the beneficiary gets is income. Second, if a person is giving away a lot of money at once, it is even more important to make sure that it's given in the most effective way. So even greater expertise is required than with giving smaller amounts on a regular basis.

If you know what you are doing and if you are certain that a specific group will make the most effective use of the money, then it makes sense to give away significant chunks. But, otherwise, careful learning about how to use money well is the best way to know when that right group comes along. The "give-it-all-away" solution can be more of a cop-out on your responsibility than a noble gesture. A more sensible aim is to give it all away during your lifetime.

Minutes of Meeting

One evening last summer, a group of fifteen people assembled in a San Francisco apartment. Most of them were between twenty-five and thirty, dressed in faded blue jeans, with sneakers or hiking boots. As they drove up in Volvos, VWs, on motorcycles, or arrived on the bus, and climbed a rickety wooden staircase, carrying bags full of groceries for their communally prepared dinner, a neighbor watching would have thought it was merely a group of friends having a small party. In fact, it was quite an unusual group of people, probably the first of its kind ever to assemble in this country. That evening, its members, many of whom were strangers, had arrived from all over the United States. What they had in common was an interest in social change and the means to do something about it, that is, inherited wealth—in some cases, many millions of dollars.

This was the fifth of a series of meetings, which had been organized and run entirely by the participants. Their aim was two-fold: to discuss the most effective use of money in promoting social change and to share with each other the unusual personal problems that come with inherited wealth.

Talking about the peculiarities of our upbringing helps each of us understand why we respond to certain experiences the way we do. By providing a forum where we can share our responses to having and using money, our group has helped each of us to grow in our own way. One of the most important ways to evolve beyond a wealthy background is to give money to support the people who have had the least access to the privileges of wealth, to promote a society where there will be no vast inequities between rich and poor.

Some of us had strong feelings about not perpetuating a class structure where some people do menial work for others—work for which they are not adequately compensated. David spoke about wanting to make his daily life and his politics as compatible as possible—in other words, doing in his daily life what he espoused politically.

We wanted to get more comfortable with handling the wealth ourselves, rather than ignoring it and leaving it all up to money managers and lawyers. Some said that doing it yourself takes a lot of time and clutters your life in unnecessary and unsatisfying ways, but that the skill is a good one to have. This was especially important for the women, as it is more traditionally assumed they will hire someone to do all of their financial work for them.

We discussed when in our lives we should make a decision about giving our money away. That question hit some people the moment they inherited it, and some of them did something right away. Others just brooded about the problem and didn't know where to start. Others weren't significantly bothered by it. Some thought that it could be dysfunctional to start actively giving away money too soon, because questions about how to use money well are complicated and take time and energy. They thought it might be best to wait until other personal skills were somewhat developed.

Of course, the other side of the argument is that you have to do it in order to learn about it. To completely ignore it makes it harder in the future, and there is always the danger that you'll never get around to it.

Jeff thought that the decision-making process was really a low-level skill and that there is very little satisfaction in giving away money anyway. This led to the question of solidifying a life and career totally apart from the money, which all of us considered to be an important thing. Joanne expressed frustration about the idea of giving money away, because she didn't see good, effective things that could be done with it. It is more important for her to get her own career together before dealing with the question of giving away money. To develop an identity and some sense of satisfaction is very important. To some people, this means being paid for what you do. Wendy did not feel that her wealth was much of a pressure, because she lives entirely off the money she earns herself. There were many people, however, who were living almost entirely off their own wealth.

We discussed how to focus ourselves so that we could have a concrete influence on a particular area, given that vast problems can be most effectively dealt with if energy is directly applied. Do we fund large or small groups, locally oriented or nationally oriented? (The nationally oriented ones tend to be more interesting.)

One good goal to strive for is to develop local projects that can be replicated in other areas—or, in fact, to develop any model project that can be imitated. This is the way to get the highest leverage. Joanne spoke up in favor of going back to her home area and using money to implement model projects that have been experimented with in other parts of the country.

Some wanted to know, Do you look for projects that will improve the existing system, or do you support projects that are actively trying to change the system itself? This improve/change question is a difficult one; there are so many good, desperately needed projects that do not attempt to change the system. Our concern was how to get the most impact from a limited amount of money.

Perhaps it is more important to change ideas than to change present conditions, but often the groups most directly involved with changing ideas support massive studies that don't amount to anything. But, still, ideas have brought about significant changes, so it is best to strive for that. While ninety-five percent of the reason we got out of Vietnam was that we could not win, perhaps the other five percent was actually due to the anti-war demonstrations and the constant pressure on the government.

Someone said that the best projects should have a long-range vision of the ideal future society they are working towards, as well as a commitment to a concrete project in a specific area. So few groups have a good idea of what they are fighting for; all of their energy is taken up with what they are fighting against.

What is the perfect society? Someone suggested that decentralization of government is important, as centralization and bureaucracy are major problems for both eastern and western countries. More localized control would tend to be more responsive to people's needs. But an important thing to be wary of is that, in times of scarcity, there will be rising parochialism (groups withdrawing into themselves and not wanting to be interfered with by the outside). The desire for self-determination has to be balanced with an awareness of the good of the whole.

Jeff asserted—and others agreed—that the basis of the big picture should be an attempt to redistribute power, so that people have more control over their own lives and are less controlled by outside forces. Since the major portion of power in this country is apportioned in relation to economic wealth, this would involve a fundamental redistribution of wealth.

Any system must benefit some at the expense of others. What is the vision of an economically just society? Money equality is not the point. What is important is what people get from the society, what services they receive (health, transportation, food, etc.). Equal access to control—equal power—is the issue, not equal money.

One way that the powerless can gain power is by joining together in organizing efforts that enable them to pool their economic resources and to exert their "numbers" influence. Organizations with a lot of people can exert a surprising amount of power and can insure that an important minority viewpoint is heard. Tenants' unions are one example.

Full employment in the standard sense is not necessarily the goal. The question is how to get more meaningful work for more people. If there is not enough work to go around, then the people who can't get work should be able to satisfy their basic needs.

Perhaps people working on the least desirable jobs should be given the highest wages. It does follow that, if you get satisfaction from your job, this should be considered a part of the compensation and, consequently, you don't need that much money to make the rest of your life good. But, if your job is very menial or boring, then you have to fill in the rest of your life with something more interesting and should be given more money or material compensation.

Is philanthropy going to cause the revolution? Unlikely. In fact, how much change can actually be effected? Someone brought up the point that many of the projects that openly espouse radically changing the system can be the most phony and will either have no effect or will have a negative effect. The question should not be "How much power do we have?" but "How much can we and do we effect?" For many of us, whatever we do is an anomaly, as we are talking about exercising power and using wealth, while we more or less believe in a system where that would not be possible.

Someone asked if people would be willing to give away all of their money if the right thing came along. How committed were we to actually doing what we espoused? How much of our own security were we willing to sacrifice? Some said they could give a significant portion of their capital. Others would have to think about it.

PHILANTHROPY AS SYNERGY

Peggy Dulany

Unless one is an exhibitionist, which I am not, it is always vaguely embarrassing to talk about one's personal history and deepest motivations to persons one does not know. The motivation for doing so has to be that one thinks it will somehow mean something—make a difference—even if only by stimulating others' thinking about important issues.

My motivation is that these are not times in which any of us can afford to sit around and twiddle our thumbs. All of us are needed to make every bit of difference we can. And if talking about some of the experiences I have had, in trying to figure out how to make the difference I could make, could be helpful to you or your families in grappling with these same issues, then I will happily—or at least willingly—put my embarrassment aside.

But, to give you an idea of how deeply rooted that sense of privacy and the embarrassment resulting from losing any of it is, here is a vignette from every day of my elementary school years in New York. Because we were six children attending two different schools, my parents bought a large Chrysler "hearse," as we referred to it, or limousine, as it would be called more conventionally. Every morning we all piled into it; the boys were dropped off at their school and then we girls at ours. We developed a deal with the chauffeur that he would stop around the corner from the school, so that no one would see us emerging from this embarrassingly large car. Meanwhile, from two blocks away, we would hide on the floor of the back seat and, when the car got to the appointed corner, we would dart out and get away from it as quickly as possible. It must have been quite a sight, seeing this apparently empty car pull up and four small uniformed girl creatures suddenly pop out of it!

I don't know whether this early consciousness of something being different was good or bad. It was certainly uncomfortable. But I think it was perhaps the roots of a social conscience, for which I give credit to both of my parents. My father was more conventionally oriented to philanthropy, having been brought up—and having brought us up—with the notion that having more money than other people implied a responsibility to give part of it away. From our earliest Sunday School days, we gave ten percent of our allowance to the collection plate. Giving away money to causes was a regular topic of conversation, and I don't think it ever occurred to any of the six of us not to do it.

But, in some ways, I credit my mother even more than my father with influencing the direction and depth of the commitment to making a difference that my siblings and I share. My mother was not from a wealthy family and had a horror of our growing up as spoiled little rich kids. She did everything she could to let us grow up as regular kids (and clearly instilled in us the desire to be so— witness our reaction to the chauffeured limousine!). I know it was not always easy for our parents, because normalcy in the late fifties and the sixties was not what had been normal for them. An example: when I was in high school at a private boarding school, a favorite teacher initiated an exchange between some of us and students at the Benjamin Franklin High School at 116th Street in New York. On our spring vacation, during which Franklin was in session, eight or ten of us went to visit their senior honors class. Being kids, we quickly struck up a relationship and spent the afternoon visiting different areas of East Harlem—El Mercado, some stores, and the apartment of one of the kids. After a complicated reciprocal visit, during which a few of the visitors felt they were being racially discriminated against by other students at my school, the friendships deepened. My brother's and my normal reaction was to invite the four students with whom we had become friends to visit us for a weekend in Maine. This seemed simple enough to us—my father had recently purchased a plane on which he flew up to Bar Harbor on weekends, so we didn't need to worry about the cost factor for them.

Initially my parents said no. It would be uncomfortable for the kids, they said, and too big a leap for them to make. To their credit, they were able to hear our arguments that this was inconsistent with what we had been taught: we invited other friends to visit with no problem, so why not these?

The weekend had all the tensions, wonderful moments, and complications that one would expect from any intercultural experience. My mother kept a picture of Gloria (one of the girls) and me sailing off to nowhere on a half-submerged homemade raft for many years, years after Gloria and I had lost touch. I later learned that my father had anonymously put all four of our visitors through college and had kept track of them through their high school counselor.

This is only a vignette, but it seems more relevant this week than it did ten days ago, with the intervening events in Los Angeles and the obvious need for communication, understanding, and outreach. I reflect on this experience as I bring up my fifteen-year-old son and worry about his going to school in a very homogeneous community outside Cincinnati.

Perhaps that experience was part of what led me to accept an invitation extended by friends of my parents to spend a summer with them in Brazil; I accepted on the condition that I could "do something useful." That started an odyssey that was probably the key formative experience of my life. Between the ages of seventeen and twenty-one, I spent a total of nearly a year in Rio, initially living with the family that invited me and working in one of the squatter settlements, or *favelas*, and eventually moving into a settlement for a couple of months to live with a family I had come to know there. Would you have let your nineteen-year-old daughter do that? Needless to say, it was not easy convincing my parents that this was a good idea. But again, they eventually went along with it and, when my father visited Brazil later that summer as part of his travels with Chase Manhattan Bank, he found the time to come with me to visit the family with whom I was staying. The ultimate irony was that the doorman at the fancy hotel where I spent a night with my father was my next door neighbor in Jacarezinho. We made sure he got to deliver the flowers that came to the suite, so he would have an excuse to come up and say hello.

The privacy issue came up during that period too. It got around in the social circles in Rio, to which my original host family belonged, that I was living in a *favela*, something that was unimaginable to most of them, but which was viewed as a good story. I was actually doing anthropological field work there, trying to understand why some people who had migrated to the city, mostly from poor rural farms in the interior of the country, could cope with modern city life, while others could not. So I was spending my days interviewing people. One day, to my horror, one of my colleagues came rushing into the house where I was in the middle of an interview, to tell me there was a *Journal do Brasil* truck wending its way up the only navigable road in the *favela*, blaring over its loudspeaker the message that they knew there was a Rockefeller there somewhere and they would pay for information about her. I was told to leave immediately so that I wouldn't entirely ruin the research. The experience was, to say the least, very traumatic, and ultimately led to my changing my name from Rockefeller to Dulany, which had been my middle name. At a time when I was just beginning to get my bearings as an individual and to find my path in life, I was suddenly faced with the stark realization that, even if I felt like—and tried to live like—a normal person (although some would have questioned the normalcy of some of my behavior!), I was not going to be treated as normal, because of the circumstances of my birth.

It took a good ten years more to come to terms with this fact and to be willing to build on what I had, rather than hide from it. During six of those years I ran an alternative high school for dropout students under the name Dulany. When I moved back to New York and went to work with my father at The New York City Partnership (a public-private partnership that tries to address the economic and social problems of New York City by bringing together labor, business, government, and community groups to develop solutions jointly), I came to see that being known as my father's daughter could sometimes be a useful factor and did not have to be misused.

But what does all this have to do with philanthropy? In my view, philanthropy is an extension of one's values, and one's values grow out of one's experience and upbringing. I can only understand my own motivations and behavior if I look back at key formative experiences. And I have found it useful to talk about these formative experiences with my son, as he begins to reach out and make decisions about what he wants to do.

My own philanthropy has been a gradually evolving process—and I'm sure the process is not finished yet. Shortly after I turned twenty-one, I began to be invited to sit on boards of trustees, mostly—in those early years—of institutions of higher education. Participating on those boards was a real learning experience for me. I learned a lot about management and about fundraising. Cambridge College and I grew up together, as person and institution. (Cambridge College is a unique program for adults without access to traditional institutions of higher learning that is dedicated to helping people be more effective in community service, whether as teachers, managers, counselors, or administrators.) In the sixteen years I have served on the Cambridge College board as member and chair, it has grown from a small, indebted institution with 150 students to a flourishing, multi-faceted college in the middle of an endowment campaign and with a student body of over 1,000. Its president and I went on our first fundraising visits together, quaking in our high-heeled shoes—and critiquing our performances afterwards. We were miserable failures at first, but we got better. If we hadn't, we wouldn't be over halfway through a $15 million campaign!

Of course, I was also asked to give my own money. It is not surprising that the most satisfying gifts were to those organizations with which I was most closely involved. Strange as it may seem, the structure of my family's generational trusts did not leave my generation initially as wealthy as popular myth would have it. One of the things with which I have had to struggle was the often evident disappointment with the size of the gift I was able to make, even to the institutions about which I cared the most. Being able to contribute in other ways, such as through assistance with fundraising, was therefore doubly satisfying.

But where things really came together for me, between the values and the action, the philanthropy and the work, was when I founded The Synergos Institute almost six years ago. You have heard a little about my early experiences in Brazil. What I did not mention was how marked and impressed I was by the amazing capacity of people with almost no material resources to make something of their lives by working in close association with community organizations—whether those be related to religion, neighborhood, recreation, or economic development. Later I worked in a public school system and saw how crippling bureaucracy can be, yet how necessary some form of centralized organization is to make large systems work. And when I worked at The New York City Partnership, I began to see the potential for tapping that local, creative community energy, while tying it to the resources and skills of business, labor, and government to solve problems.

Synergos is an organization, but it is also a dream. It is founded on the principle of synergy: the complementary action of different agents together creates a whole greater than the sum of the separate parts. I am convinced that, in a world as complex as that we live in, each of us must be a catalytic agent for the good of the whole, in whatever way we can—whether at the neighborhood, city, national, or international level.

Synergos was founded with the idea that people and groups can work together to solve problems and that, in doing so, those problems get solved more effectively and permanently, because everyone has an investment in the joint solution. I didn't set out to work in Brazil again, but it's probably not a coincidence that one of the places where we participated in forming a partnership to address the staggering issue of child poverty was in Rio, where I had lived twenty years before. And it certainly is not a coincidence that this partnership takes its lead from issues identified by the youth themselves and their families, stimulating their energy and commitment to find a solution, while bringing other groups with different resources to the table as well. Yesterday, the Minister of Education and Environment of Brazil, whom I had met in February, called our office to say that the President of the Bank of Brazil was willing to put a half million dollars into a fund to train youths for jobs, if matching funds could be found. But he wasn't quite sure how to go about it. Could we help? Of course we will put him in touch with groups in Brazil already doing this, trying to match resources with skills, goodwill with energy. That is the nature of the synergy we are seeking.

In addition to being the president and founder, I am also a funder of Synergos, putting half of all my philanthropic dollars into it each year—part for operating expenses and part toward an endowment fund. In the beginning, my gift was a large part of the budget; now it is less than one-tenth. If that were not the case, I would not be following my own principles of promoting self-reliance, because an organization should never depend on only one source.

Condensing into a couple of paragraphs a process that took over twenty years to evolve seems ludicrous, but I want to make the point that one's philanthropy grows out of one's life experience and, at its most satisfying, is linked to one's life commitment. On the one hand, the direction that it takes is inevitably highly personal, because no one else can live your life. On the other hand, we are all on Spaceship Earth together, and it is in each of our interests that our stay here be as harmonious, as productive, and as protective of our "ship" for our grandchildren as possible.

I am grateful to my parents that they helped me expand my definition of the Spaceship past midtown Manhattan—first to East Harlem, then to Brazil, and from there to the world as a whole. I am trying to do the same for my son. I am convinced that that is the greatest gift we can give our children, for that instills in them a feeling of interconnectedness, a sense of commitment, and a drive to make things better. From that, philanthropy will follow as a natural consequence.

TOWARDS A NEW PHILANTHROPY: EXPANDING WEALTHY INDIVIDUAL AND FAMILY GIVING IN THE 1990S

Stanley Salett

A s the United States lurches toward the 21st century, at times at war and constantly in debt, some attention is being given again to the poor. And as we begin again to study the lives of the poor, their culture, and their living conditions, this time we should also consider the lives and culture of those at the other end of the economic strata—the wealthy.

Robert Coles, after embarking on his well-admired series, *Children of Crisis*, which focused on children of the poor from several racial and cultural groups, was asked by some of the poor families he interviewed how he was "doing with the rich folks . . . the ones who decide how the poor folks live."[1]

With such prodding, Coles decided somewhat hesitatingly to devote his fifth and final volume to the children of wealth.

> Why indeed shouldn't a "study" of the lives of poor, vulnerable, harassed children also include a consideration of the purposes, aims, ideas and feelings of those "others" so removed apparently by "station" in life, yet so involved by virtue of the money they have, the positions they occupy, the authority they possess and wield, the influence they exert?[2]

It is one of the assumptions of this essay that the problems of poverty and other great issues confronting this country cannot be addressed adequately without a thorough consideration of wealth in America and without the involvement of the wealthy themselves. What is needed is a deeper understanding of what it means to have wealth and, most importantly, of how the philanthropic instincts of a new generation of the wealthy can be extended and strengthened.[3]

Most public and private attention to the expansion of philanthropy tends to focus on the agents and institutions of organized giving: foundations, corporate giving programs, associations of foundations, and regional associations of grantmakers. Attention to individual giving is assumed to be the province of the United Way or alternative giving programs like the Black United Way. The lack of emphasis on encouraging, extending, and improving larger scale individual and family philanthropy is particularly unfortunate, because the largest potential growth in philanthropy in the next two decades is likely to come from individuals and families. Support of the nonprofit sector from individual and family giving has grown more rapidly than from any other source.

In 1991, the most recent year reported on, a total of $124.77 billion was given to nonprofit organizations by private, nongovernmental sources. Of this amount, $7.76 billion (6.2 percent) came from foundations, $6.1 billion (4.9 percent) from corporations, and the remaining $110.91 billion (88.9 percent) from individuals and families. When bequests are subtracted from the overall figure, the rate of growth in individual and family giving over the previous year was 6.8 percent, or 1.93 in constant terms.[4]

The post-World War II generation of Americans, the "baby boomers," can expect to inherit more wealth in the next two decades than any other generation in the history of the world. According to a recent study conducted by Cornell University's Department of Economics and Housing, "64 million baby boomers stand to inherit 6.8 trillion dollars between 1987 and 2011."[5] The study also predicted that the richest 1 percent of this generation (640,000 individuals) will inherit one-third of the total, or an average of 3.6 million dollars each.

The use of these funds will obviously have a great impact on the country. Will the nineties and beyond see a continuation of high acquisition lifestyles? Will federal and state governments seek to increase taxes on this unprecedented personal wealth? Will there be an increase in charitable giving and public interest sector support? The answers will affect us all.

Some observers have noted what they believe to be a withdrawal of the wealthy from public participation and support for public needs. They describe the growing propensity of the wealthy to live in suburban and urban enclaves, protected by private security, their children educated in private schools, their recreation provided by private clubs and, for some, even their trash collection and streetcleaning "privatized" by paying extra taxes for additional service.[6]

As the eighties were marked by increased privatization of services for the wealthy, it was also a period of reduced charitable giving by the very rich. Taxpayers earning more than $500,000 reduced their average donations from $47,432 in 1980 to $16,062 in 1988.[7]

The last decade has also seen a dramatic concentration of wealth and a growth in the number of individual fortunes in the United States.[8] In 1980, there were 574,000 millionaires;[9] in 1992, 2,320,000.[10] In 1982, 38,885 individual household fortunes were at least 10 million dollars;[11] in 1988, there were at least 100,000 at that level.[12] Between 1982 and 1992, the number of centimillionaires grew from 400[13] to 2,560,[14] and the number of billionaires from 13[15] to 73.[16] According to data compiled by the Federal Reserve Board in 1992, the share of net wealth held by the richest 1 percent of United States households in 1989 was 37 percent, up from 31 percent in 1983.[17]

Most Americans hold wealth in the forms of homes, automobiles, furnishings, appliances, and cash. A small minority own corporate stock or commercial real estate, and even fewer own corporate or municipal bonds or treasury bills. However, the top 1 percent of wealthholders hold 49 percent of all publicly traded stock, 62 percent of business assets, 78 percent of bonds and trusts, and 45 percent of all non-residential real estate.[18]

In 1992, there were 475,000 super-rich households, the top 0.5 percent of the population. The average net worth of the group was $5.1 million, and the lowest amount of household wealth was $2.96 million. The next 475,000, or second 0.5 percent of the population, the very rich, had net worths between approximately $2.14 and $2.95 million, with an average wealth per household of $2.52 million.[19]

In his book *The Politics of Rich and Poor: Wealth and the American Electorate in the Reagan Aftermath,* Kevin Phillips foresees a coming period of populism and increased taxation of the rich as an inevitable reaction against these concentrations of great wealth. The historical precedents are clear. At the turn of the century, during the first populist/progressive period, President Theodore Roosevelt called for increasing taxes on the rich. In his message to Congress on December 3, 1906, Roosevelt urged that "the prime object should be to put an increasing burden on these swollen fortunes which it is certainly no benefit to this country to perpetuate."[20]

A second Roosevelt president sounded a similar theme during the second populist/progressive period. On June 19, 1935, Franklin Roosevelt said:

> The transmission from generation to generation of vast fortunes by will, inheritance or gift is not consistent with ideals and sentiments of the American people. Great accumulations of wealth cannot be justified on the basis of personal or family security. Such inherited economic power is as inconsistent with the ideals of this generation as inherited political power was inconsistent with ideals of the generation which established our government.[21]

If Phillips and others who predict a new wave of populism and taxation of the wealthy in the nineties are correct, then probably not far behind will be a new wave of philanthropy. Just as the philanthropy of the new millionaires at the turn of the twentieth century followed the high point of democratic populism in the election of 1896, so the new millionaires, experiencing a surge in populist sentiment at the end of the twentieth century, may also be more inclined to give to philanthropy.

The 1986 Tax Reform Act reduced top individual income tax rates from 92 percent to 28 percent. Modified in 1990, top individual rates were still, at 31 percent, at the historical lower end. The effect of the 1986 Act was to reduce taxes for all income classes, but the lowest income groups received the smallest cut. Although the wealthy received a proportionately higher benefit from reduced taxes, their incentive for charitable giving was considerably reduced.[22]

More recently there have been renewed calls for increased taxation of the wealthy by raising marginal income tax rates, increasing estate taxes, or creating new sources of taxation such as a wealth tax.[23] Several countries tax wealth directly. France and The Netherlands tax wealthy individuals only. West Germany has a net worth tax on individuals and corporations. Switzerland taxes the net wealth of individuals and places a capital tax on corporate equity.

TABLE I
COUNTRIES THAT TAX WEALTH AND THEIR
WEALTH TAX RATES (1987)[24]

COUNTRY	TAX RATES (%)
Argentina	1.5
France	1.5
Germany	.5
India	.5 to 5.0
Indonesia	.5
Italy	.5 to 2.0
Netherlands	1.5
Sweden	1.5 to 3.0
Switzerland	.17 to 1.0

Whatever form it takes, taxation of the wealthy will likely be greater in the nineties than in the eighties. If the charitable deduction remains in effect, then there will be even more incentive to give in the years ahead.

Who are the new super-rich and what are their philanthropic tendencies? Turn-of-the-century fortunes of oil and steel created the philanthropic bases of the Rockefeller and Carnegie Foundations. From the 1920s until the end of World War II, traditional industries in manufacturing and natural resources development continued to form the bases of substantial foundations: Pew (oil), Kaiser (heavy industry), and Kettering, Mott, Sloan, Ford (automobiles).[25] Following World War II, other consumer-related industries such as pharmaceuticals (Johnson, Lilly) developed large foundations. Since 1950, few foundations of significant size have been established. Noteworthy were: Hughes (aerospace), Ahmanson (real estate), Olin (chemicals/glass), Revson (consumer products), Annenberg, Benton, Newhouse, Wallace (broadcasting), Hewlett-Packard (high technology). While many of these individuals and families made substantial gifts and continue to do so, the sizes of their foundations do not match those of earlier periods.[26]

During the 1980s many substantial fortunes were created and expanded, but in different sectors of the economy than previously, and most new super-rich and very rich have not yet developed large philanthropic foundations like their predecessors.

Only six new foundations of more than $100 million in assets have been organized in the last three decades. And, although small foundations continue to be created, most have limited endowments ($160,000 or less). Overall, the number of foundations has continued to decline, with more than 10,000 dissolving in the last decade.[27]

Why have more foundations not been created? And what may this mean for the philanthropy of the nineties? The 1969 tax law that placed unprecedented restrictions and reporting requirements on foundations was obviously a factor in terminating many foundations in the following years, but other factors must also be examined.

For all of the attention paid to philanthropy, much is presumed—but surprisingly little is known—about the motivations of the wealthy to give. To a great extent, the philanthropy of the next twenty-five years will be defined by the giving patterns of the baby boom generation. Born between 1946 and 1964, it is the largest generation in United States history.[28] And, as the baby boomers have aged, they have left few sectors of our society and culture unchanged.

> As children they heard stories about how the schools and colleges were overcrowded because of them (enrollment in United States schools increased 52 percent between 1950 and 1960); as adolescents they found many of their elders emulating what they wore and dancing to their music; and as adults, their enormous buying power would determine what was 'in' for the whole culture. *Time* magazine, in the 1960s, would even make them its "Man of the Year."[29]

Early predictions of the baby boom generation shifting the country dramatically to the left, politically and culturally, have been unfulfilled.[30] Later analysts of the baby boom generation have seen greater complexity in this generation. To assume that a generation is shaped by a common core of experience may cause us to minimize the importance of the differing ages at which individuals in the baby boom generation experienced the impact of the Vietnam War or the space shuttle disaster.[31]

Other divisions among baby boomers most certainly and obviously exist. Baby boomers divide along lines of race, class, ethnicity, gender, and geography. One recent analyst described the generation by creating categories of:

> ...the pleasure seekers—who are striving to enjoy life; the competitors—who are business- and profession-obsessed; the trapped—who are in difficult situations at home or at work, and who cannot bring themselves to get out; the contented—who are generally satisfied with their lives; and the "get highs"—who are excessively involved in alcohol and drugs or even, many baby boomers insist, in matters of the spirit.[32]

Yet this is a generation whose differences from those generations born both before and after have been stressed continually throughout their lifetimes. This was the first generation to be singled out by commercial advertising for special attention, beginning in the 1950s and building through the 1960s. And the primary medium of the message that the baby boom generation was special was television.

> Marketing, and especially television, isolated their needs and their wants from those of their parents. From the cradle, the baby boomers had been surrounded by products created especially for them, from silly putty to slinkys to skate boards. New products, new toys, new commercials, new fads—the dictatorship of the new—was integral to the baby boom experience. So prevalent was it that the baby boomers themselves rarely realized how different it made them. They breathed it like air.[33]

It is, then, a segment of this so self-consciously different generation that will define philanthropy for themselves and, to a considerable extent, for the rest of us. The new philanthropy will have other nongenerational influences to be sure, such as tax policies, populist anti-wealth movements, and the attitudes of younger generations towards privileges and position in society.

The new philanthropy has already begun to show itself in the alternative fund movement, feminists' and women's foundations, and the first philanthropic networks, some organized on an international scale. The first alternative fund to be organized was the Vanguard Public Foundation in the early 1970s. The six founders were all baby boomers between the ages of twenty-two and twenty-six. One early donor described this different way of giving:

> The appeal of Vanguard was that it was a group of peers trying to do something . . . really moving philanthropy in a different direction, providing resources to the kind of ideas, beliefs, values that we shared. And it was a cooperative enterprise at that point, even though we were donor-controlled. It was a group of donors that wasn't related by family, which was sort of a new thing.[34]

Through the work of George Pillsbury, heir to the baking goods company, and others, there are presently about twenty alternative funds or giving programs in the United States. While there is no one model, most funds have been initiated by members of the baby boom generation. They have established a network of "rich kids" bound together by family, school, and class ties. Together, several of these new philanthropy activists organized ARF (amalgamated rich folks), a national organization of wealthy donors, and the funding exchange, a national umbrella group of alternative funds.[35] On the average, a new alternative fund has been created every year since the early 1970s; altogether, over the course of fifteen years, these funds have distributed more than $30 million.[36]

Other examples of new philanthropic organizations initiated since 1970 include:

- The **Partnership for Democracy:** Supports community organization and economic democracy through grants and donor advisor funds;

- The **Threshold Foundation:** Gives approximately $1 million annually through more than 200 wealthy donors;

- The **Peace Development Fund and Ploughshares:** Both supported by individual donors who pool their funds to support organizations working on peace, disarmament, and other foreign policy issues;

- The **Territory Resource:** Pools the funds of 30+ donors, who give in the $3,500 to $30,000/year range;

- The **Seventh Generation Fund:** Donor-supported grants and technical assistance to Native American communities.[37]

Whether the more recently arrived, self-made, super-wealthy members of the baby boom generation will also participate in alternative funds, or create other philanthropic vehicles for themselves, or refuse to give at all is yet to be seen. Again, there has been surprisingly little written and no systematic inquiry about the philanthropic inclinations of the newly wealthy. Alan Rabinowitz notes that "No one has speculated on the willingness of the new stock market and high technology billionaires to fund progressive social change activities."[38]

While many of the characteristics of the baby boom generation are speculative, one is certain. The boom generation in its later years will be increasingly composed of females who will be increasingly alone.[39] By the year 2000, there will be half again more women than men over sixty-five. Largely due to the higher death rate of men throughout their lives, women begin to outnumber men by age twenty-five.

The feminization of poverty is but one effect of this phenomenon. Another is that women of wealth will have much greater influence in the new philanthropy. There are now more than forty women's foundations in the United States. The first one, The Women's Foundation, began in San Francisco. Formed in the early 1980s, it is organized as a public foundation to give money to projects for women and girls. Since its creation, The Women's Foundation has granted $900,000.[40]

One of the founders of The Women's Foundation, Tracy Duvivier Gary, described its beginnings. "We really wanted to create an organization that could be a catalyst for involvement for a whole new generation of people, women specifically, who would be interested in philanthropy."[41] It is this sense of personal involvement and participation that is one of the prime characteristics of the new philanthropy, and it is likely that these new patterns of personal involvement in charitable giving will continue to grow.

The role of baby boom women of wealth in initiating and sustaining so many of these new philanthropic ventures is particularly noteworthy. The tradition in which women of wealth have set the private social welfare standards of the United States is continuing. [42]

For women of wealth, assuming more control over their own philanthropic (and, by extension, financial) decisions has not been easy. Upper class women by tradition have turned over their inheritances to their husbands to manage.[43] Changing this pattern for most women, particularly those of an earlier generation, is difficult. Susan Ostrander observes that "women . . . ultimately have to challenge the men's class position in society in order to manage their own money. Upper class men . . . exercise the dominant economic and political power in the society. It is unlikely that they would relinquish such power in their own families or that their wives would be able to seriously challenge it."[44] While Ostrander's study of upper-class women is of a pre-baby boom generation, the conditions she describes have not disappeared.

Another characteristic of the new philanthropy is an increasing focus on international issues. Consider a recently organized group named "Partners." Partners describes itself as a "global team of men and women from diverse backgrounds, nationalities and professions," who are working on problems of demilitarization, development, and the environment. Their prospectus states:

> Every generation approaches global problems within the framework of its own era. *Partners* is a concept of a different generation, within a new framework. It is not governmental, but independent. Not national, but transnational. Not large, but small. Not bureaucratic, but flexible and fast moving.[45]

Compare this approach with the traditional philanthropy of the earlier generation. Their focus has been on the near at hand and the familiar, on institutions with which they or their families have been associated—museums, hospitals, private schools, colleges and universities. As an established Eastern philanthropist described his giving,

> I would say, in terms of dollar volume, that 90% of what I do each year is given to the organizations with which I am directly associated. The other 10% are small gifts to local community things that need support but do not need massive amounts from any individuals such as myself. . . . I tend to give to organizations that I know the most about, the ones I personally serve.[46]

Within American society, the disposition of wealth has changed considerably from one generation to the next. What causes one generation to display its wealth more, or pass less of it on to their children and grandchildren, or give more or less to charity are all interesting questions, essentially unexplored and concealed behind the popular stories and myths of the "rich and famous."[47]

However, as ill-defined as it may be, a new philanthropy has begun to emerge. Its language, concepts, and philanthropic vehicles are substantially different from earlier forms. These new philanthropic organizations are described most frequently as "exchanges"

77

or "networks" or "partnerships," terms implying a sharing among equals and participatory models of decision-making. Most of these new forms are also intended to be nonbureaucratic, nonhierarchical, and less sexist than earlier counterparts.

To date, despite their energy and innovation, the new philanthropic organizations of the last two decades have not succeeded in attracting significant participation from the baby boom generation's wealthy or their wealthy predecessors. When one considers that the Forbes 400 increased their net worth from $92 billion in 1982 to $300.7 billion in 1992, the growth of new philanthropy seems very modest indeed.[48]

There are some positive signs and some mixed signals about whether the wealthy will give more in the future. A survey conducted for the Independent Sector by the Gallup organization and reported on in the fall of 1990 showed the baby boom generation with the biggest increases in contributions and in volunteering their time, in comparison with older generations. However, the same survey reported that the less affluent were more generous than the very wealthy.[49]

What is clear is that there is no systematic effort by the nonprofit sector or anyone else to reach the wealthy of this emerging generation—with its unprecedented fortune—to encourage it to greater philanthropy. Every generation provides its own set of responses to wealth and poverty. The responses of the baby boom generation should be known by the year 2016, when the oldest members turn seventy and the youngest fifty-two. To turn the wealthiest segment of that generation toward greater giving is a task worthy of our best organized and systematic efforts. We should do no less.

NOTES

1. Robert Coles, *The Privileged Ones: The Well-Off and the Rich in America* (Boston: Little, Brown, 1977), x.

2. Ibid., xi-xii.

3. What is wealth? Perhaps a question for the ages. Wealth is often confused with income. Yet a family can make great income without being wealthy. Obversely, wealthy families may at times have little or no income. Wealth can be most easily understood as stored up purchasing power, the net value of which can be obtained from one's holdings once all debts and liabilities have been eliminated.

4. *Giving U.S.A.: The Annual Report on Philanthropy for the Year 1991*, ed., Ann E. Kaplan, (New York: American Association of Fund Raising Counsel Trust for Philanthropy, 1992), 20.

5. *New York Times*, July 22, 1990, Section E, 4.

6. Robert B. Reich, "Secession of the Successful," *The New York Times Magazine*, January 20, 1991, 17.

7. Ibid., 18.

8. Kevin Phillips, *The Politics of Rich and Poor: Wealth and the American Electorate in the Reagan Aftermath* (New York: Random House, 1990), Appendix A.

9. Ibid.

10. "PSI's 1992 Affluent Market Consumer Survey" (Tampa: PSI, 1993)

11. Phillips, *The Politics of Rich and Poor.*

12. Thomas T. Stanley, *Marketing to the Affluent* (Homewood, IL: Dow Jones-Irwin, 1988).

13. Phillips, *The Politics of Rich and Poor.*

14. "PSI's 1992 Affluent Market Consumer Survey."

15. Phillips, *The Politics of Rich and Poor.*

16. "The Richest People in America," *Forbes,* October 19, 1992.

17. *New York Times*, April 21, 1992, Sec. A, 1.

18. Ibid, 17.

19. "PSI's 1992 Affluent Market Consumer Survey." The net worth figures in this paragraph do not include principal residence.

20. Gustave Myers, *The Ending of Hereditary American Fortunes* (New York: Julian Messner, 1939), 370; citing the *Congressional Record,* 59th Cong., 2d sess., 27-28.

21. Ibid., citing the *Congressional Record,* 74th Cong., 1st sess., pt. 9 (House ex. doc. No. 229), 9,657.

22. Center on Budget and Policy Priorities, *Smaller Slices of the Pie* (Washington, D.C., 1985), 4.

23. William M. Dugger, "The Wealth Tax: A Policy Proposal," *Journal of Economic Issues,* 24 (March 1990), 140-144. A recent U.S. proposal for a wealth tax begins with the assumption that of the entire population, 4,377,000 individuals have wealth (gross assets of $300,000 or more) and collectively hold about $3,300 billion net worth. If a personal deduction of $300,000 were granted to each wealth holder, that would leave a taxable wealth base of $1,934 billion. A suggested tax rate of 8.0 percent would yield $155 billion, about enough to cover half of the most recent projected federal deficit.

24. M. W. E. Glautier, *A Reference Guide to International Taxation* (Lexington: D. C. Heath and Co., 1987), 109-117.

25. Robert Heilbronner comments that "had Henry and Edsel Ford's wealth not gone to a philanthropic foundation, their estate taxes would have amounted to over $300,000,000." Robert L. Heilbronner, *The Quest for Wealth: A Study of Acquisitive Man* (New York: Simon and Schuster, 1956), 220.

26. Jacqueline Thompson, *Future Rich: The People, Companies and Industries Creating America's Next Fortunes* (New York: William Morrow, 1985), 16-19.

27. Teresa Odendahl, "Independent Foundations and Wealthy Donors: An Overview," in *America's Wealthy and the Future of Foundations,* ed. Teresa Odendahl (New York: Foundation Center, 1987), 2-4.

28. 3,400,000 babies were born in 1946, an increase of 20 percent over the previous year. Births peaked at 4,300,000 in 1957 and stayed above 4,000,000 a year through 1964. See Jerry Gerber et al., *Lifetrends: The Future of Baby Boomers and Other Aging Americans* (New York: Macmillan, 1989), 13.

29. Ibid.

30. See, for example, Charles Reich: "This is a revolution of the new generation, their protest and rebellion, their culture, clothes, music, drugs, ways of thought and liberated life style. . . . We can see that the present transformation goes beyond anything in modern history." Charles Reich, *The Greening of America* (New York: Random House, 1970), 242-243.

31. Michael S. Delli Carpini, *Stability and Change in American Politics: The Coming of Age of the Generation of the 1960s* (New York: NYU Press, 1986), 11.

32. Daniel Quinn Mills, *Not Like Our Parents: How the Baby Boom Generation is Changing America* (New York: Morrow, 1987), 17.

33. Landon Jones, *Great Expectations: America and the Baby Boom Generation* (New York: Coward-McCann, 1980), 43.

34. Quoted in Teresa Odendahl, *Charity Begins at Home: Generosity and Self-Interest among the Philanthropic Elite* (New York: Basic Books, 1990), 174.

35. Ibid., 172.

36. Ibid., 180.

37. Cynthia Guyer, *Developing New Sources of Progressive Philanthropy: New Donors from New Constituencies* (Unpublished paper, November, 1990), 11.

38. Alan Rabinowitz, *Social Change Philanthropy in America* (Westport: Quorum Books, 1990).

39. Jones, *Great Expectations,* 320.

40. Odendahl, *Charity Begins at Home,* 187-193.

41. Ibid., 192.

42. G. William Domhoff, *The Higher Circles: The Governing Class in America* (New York: Random House, 1970), 34-35.

43. See Susan A. Ostrander, *Women of the Upper Class* (Philadelphia: Temple University Press, 1984), 65.

44. Ibid., 66.

45. *Partners: A Global Action Team,* unpublished prospectus (Santa Monica: Partners, November 15, 1988).

46. Odendahl, *Charity Begins at Home,* 23.

47. See John J. DeMarco and Kaki Denner, "Examining Dramatic Growth in the Affluent Market," *Trusts and Estates,* (October 1990), 16. In their continuing study of the affluent market, DeMarco and Denner found a growing number of wealthy less likely to pass their assets to their heirs.

48. Kevin Phillips, "Bush's Domestic Policy? It's Soak the Middle Class," *Los Angeles Times,* February 24, 1991, M6.

49. In 1989, households with incomes under $10,000 gave 5.5.% of their income to charities, while those with incomes of $50,000 to $60,000 gave 1.7%; those earning $75,000 to $100,000 gave 3.2% and those earning more than $100,000 gave 2.9%. Beverly Bayette, "Is Philanthropy's Clock 'Ticking Away'?," *Los Angeles Times,* October 25, 1990.

Stanley Salett

Bibliography

Aldrich, Nelson W., Jr. *Old Money: The Mythology of America's Upper Class.* New York: Knopf, 1988.

Allen, Michael Patrick. *The Founding Fortunes: A New Anatomy of the Super-Rich Families in America.* New York: Dutton, 1987.

Boissevain, Jeremy. *Friends of Friends: Networks, Manipulators and Coalitions.* Oxford: Blackwell, 1974.

Center on Budget and Policy Priorities. *Smaller Slices of the Pie.* Washington, D.C., 1985.

Casale, Anthony M. *Where Have All the Flowers Gone? The Fall and the Rise of the Baby Boom Generation.* Kansas City: Andreos and McMeel, 1989.

Coles, Robert. *The Privileged Ones: The Well-Off and the Rich in America.* Boston: Little, Brown, 1977.

Delli Carpini, Michael X. *Stability and Change in American Politics: The Coming of Age of the Generation of the 1960s.* New York: New York University Press, 1986.

DeMarco, John J. and Kaki Denner. "Examining Dramatic Growth in the Affluent Market." *Trusts and Estates.* October 1990.

Domhoff, G. William. *The Higher Circles: The Governing Class in America.* New York: Vintage, 1970.

Dugger, William M. "The Wealth Tax: A Policy Proposal." *Journal of Economic Issues*, March 24, 1990: 140-144.

Gerber, Jerry et al. *Lifetrends: The Future of Baby Boomers and Other Aging Americans.* New York: Macmillan, 1989.

Gerzon, Mark. *The Whole World is Watching: A Young Man Looks at Youth's Dissent.* New York: Viking, 1969.

Glautier, M.W.E. *A Reference Guide to International Taxation.* Lexington: D.C. Heath, 1987.

Guyer, Cynthia. *Developing New Sources of Progressive Philanthropy: New Donors from New Constituencies.* Unpublished paper, November 1990.

Heilbronner, Robert L. *The Quest for Wealth: A Study of Acquisitive Man.* New York: Simon and Schuster, 1956.

Joint Economic Committee. *The Concentration of Wealth in the United States: Trends in the Distribution of Wealth among American Families.* Washington, D.C.: United States Congress, 1986.

Jones, Landon Y. *Great Expectations: America and the Baby Boom Generation.* New York: Coward-McCann, 1980.

Kirstein, George G. *The Rich: Are They Different?* Boston: Houghton Mifflin, 1968.

Light, Paul C. *Baby Boomers.* New York: Norton, 1988.

Mills, D. Quinn. *Not Like Our Parents: How the Baby Boom Generation Is Changing America.* New York: Morrow, 1987.

Myers, Gustave. *The Ending of Hereditary American Fortunes.* New York: Julian Messner, 1939.

Odendahl, Teresa. *Charity Begins at Home: Generosity and Self-Interest among the Philanthropic Elite.* New York: Basic Books, 1990.

"Independent Foundations and Wealthy Donors: An Overview." *America's Wealthy and the Future of Foundations.* New York: Foundation Center (1987): 27-42.

Ostrander, Susan A. *Women of the Upper Class.* Philadelphia: Temple University, 1984.

Partners. *Partners: A Global Action Team.* Unpublished prospectus. Santa Monica, 1November 15, 1988.

Pear, Robert. "Rich Got Richer in 80s: Others Held Even." *New York Times* (national). January 11, 1991, A1, A20.

Phillips, Kevin. *The Politics of Rich and Poor: Wealth and the American Electorate in the Reagan Aftermath.* New York: Random House, 1990.

Rabinowitz, Alan. *Social Change Philanthropy in America.* Westport, CT: Quorum Books, 1990.

Ravo, Nick. "A Windfall Nears in Inheritances from the Richest Generation." *New York Times,* July 22, 1990, E4.

Reich, Charles. *The Greening of America.* New York: Random House, 1970.

Reich, Robert B. "Secession of the Successful." *New York Times Magazine.* January 20, 1991, 42-45.

Smith, James D. *The Concentration of Wealth in the United States.* Washington, D.C.: Joint Economic Committee, U.S. Congress, 1986.

Stanley, Thomas J. *Marketing to the Affluent.* Homewood, IL: Dow-Jones Irwin, 1988.

Thompson, Jacqueline. *Future Rich: The People, Companies and Industries Creating America's Next Fortunes.* New York: William Morrow, 1985.

United Way of America. *What Lies Ahead: Countdown to the 21st Century.* Alexandria: United Way of America, 1989.

Weber, Nathan, ed. *Giving USA: The Annual Report of Philanthropy for the Year 1989.* New York: American Association of Fund Raising Counsel, 1990.

PHILANTHROPY AS A MORAL
IDENTITY OF *CARITAS*

Paul G. Schervish

The foregoing essays have articulated several practical aspects of what it means to take giving seriously. We have heard what the conference participants had to say about the considerations they take into account in carrying out their philanthropy. We have also heard directly from four of the participants either about their own philanthropic resume or about the contemporary social context facing the wealthy philanthropist. Always implicit and often explicit in these essays is the notion that *serious* philanthropic engagement is much more than a matter of economics or social status. There are, of course, many wealthy individuals who neglect philanthropy altogether or who carry it out in a nonchalant or self-serving manner. But for those who take giving seriously—both in the extent of their financial commitment and the depth of their concern—philanthropy has become an integral part of their moral identity. Serious philanthropists— at all levels of the economic spectrum—embody a disposition of care, something too seldom acknowledged or cultivated. Drawing on the experiences enunciated in the previous essays, this chapter explores some of the philosophical and theological underpinnings of the moral identity of care, beginning with a re-examination of the definition of philanthropy.

To speak about philanthropy as a moral identity requires that we embrace a conception of philanthropy that is worthy of identity. That is, we are in search of a definition that has at its center the kinds of moral responsibilities and orientations that define character. There are, of course, many definitions of philanthropy that have been offered (see Van Til 1990), including Robert Payton's (1991) productive notion that philanthropy is "voluntary action for the public good." Some of these definitions, like Payton's, stress the voluntary nature and welfare goals of philanthropy. Other definitions focus on what is legally demarcated as charity, while still others emphasize the institutional sector in which the giving occurs. For reasons which I will clarify, none of these approaches does justice to the "inner essence" of philanthropy. What is needed is a definition that is, paradoxically, more idealistic *and* more practically grounded, one that locates the moral center of philanthropy in the exercise of the virtue of charity while, at the same time, transcending the ineluctable problem of ascertaining the boundary between self-interest and altruism.

In the following section I elaborate an understanding of philanthropy as a social relation of obligation, matching resources and needs. I differentiate philanthropy from commercial and political relations not by its "voluntary" nature or its dedication to the "public good," but by the kinds of signals or moral claims that mobilize and govern the matching of resources to needs. For the purposes of discussing philanthropy as identity, I suggest that philanthropy be defined as *the social relation in which people respond to the moral obligation to expand the boundaries of self-interest to include meeting the needs of others*. From my perspective, examining what it means to take giving seriously requires us to take seriously the meaning of giving. Perhaps this can be made clearer by discussing a scene from the musical production of *Les Miserables*.

Early in the production, the unfortunate Fantine makes a deathbed appeal to Jean Valjean to take her young daughter, Cosette, under his care:

F: My Cosette
J: Shall live in my protection
F: Take her now
J: Your child will want for nothing
F: Good Monsieur, you've come from God in Heaven
J: And none will ever harm Cosette
  as long as I am living
F: Take my hand, the night grows ever colder
J: Then I will keep you warm
F: Take my child, I give her to your keeping
J: Take shelter from the storm
F: For God's sake, please stay till I'm sleeping, and tell
  Cosette I love her and I'll see her when I wake
J: [shortly thereafter]
And this I swear to you tonight,
Your child will live within my care.
And I will raise her to the light,
I swear to you I will be there.

In this contrapuntal musical conversation we hear a personal appeal for assistance and a positive response of care. It is an epitome of what I mean by philanthropy. It includes the direct expression of need, the experience of obligation in relation to that need, and a response in which that obligation is met as a matter of self-identity. In the following comments, I will elucidate the exchange between Fantine and Jean Valjean, explaining how this represents a prototypical model of philanthropy and clarifies what it means to possess a philanthropic identity. I draw on my research with Susan Ostrander to argue that some of the most significant conceptual issues that need to be addressed in the study of giving behavior revolve around developing an understanding of philanthropy as a social relation of charity.[1] I believe that elevating the conceptual status and the ethical priority accorded the needs of recipients and the virtue of charity enhances our understanding of both the moral quality and the practical performance of philanthropy.

THE CASE FOR A NEW UNDERSTANDING

Most efforts to conceptualize philanthropy emphasize the presence of a special dedication to the public good or its voluntary nature. However, neither of these aspects gets to the essence of what distinguishes philanthropy from politics and commerce in a positive, rather than derivative, way. First, attending to the public good is not a claim that can be made exclusively on behalf of philanthropy. Commerce and politics also enjoy many moral and philosophical—not to mention ideological—arguments extolling their contribution to the public good.

To distinguish philanthropy by its "voluntary" character is equally unpersuasive. On the one hand, it is often difficult to make the case that philanthropy is actually voluntary in the sense of being sheltered from external pressures. For instance, many wealthy donors we interviewed recount the array of pressures or imperatives—business, tax, community, personal, and moral—that do, in fact, compel their philanthropic activity. On the other hand, there is a hallowed religious and ethical tradition that speaks unapologetically about the obligation of paying attention to the needs of others. Indeed, the subtitle of the conference, *The Responsibilities and Opportunities of Wealth*, explicitly recognizes this aspect of duty.

What distinguishes philanthropy is not the presence or absence of the intention to serve the public good, but the avenue for getting there. It is not the presence or absence of obligation, but what is viewed as obligating. That is, the way to distinguish philanthropic relations is by the kind of signals or claims that engage individual givers.

PHILANTHROPY, COMMERCE, AND POLITICS

I conceive of philanthropy as a particular kind of interactive production process. Philanthropy is a social relation governed by moral obligation that matches a supply of private resources to a demand of unfulfilled needs and desires. This understanding of philanthropy as a social relation of production enables us to locate the defining characteristic of philanthropy in the *type of social signals* it responds to rather than in some formal institutional characteristic such as its tax status, or some normative attribute such as its being voluntary, or some particular goal such as service for the public good.

Political activity is mobilized by the medium of political capital in the form of votes and campaign contributions. Commercial activity is mobilized by dollars or economic capital. Philanthropic activity is mobilized by moral or cultural capital in the form of symbolic expressions of need. In *commercial* relations, needs elicit a response largely to the extent that they become expressed in dollars—that is, translated into what economists call "effective demand." Similarly, in *political* relations, needs elicit a response largely to the extent that they can become expressed as campaign contributions or as votes—which, in fact, is another form of effective demand. Just what makes commercial and political demand "effective" in eliciting a response? It is that these forms of demand are presented through a medium upon which suppliers depend for their continued existence. Neither businesses nor politicians can long afford to ignore such concrete indications of their clients' will. Thus, attention to needs is generated not directly by the inherent importance of the needs themselves but indirectly by the functional importance of the medium through which the needs are expressed.

THE MEDIUM OF MORAL CLAIMS

In *philanthropic* relations, the medium for communicating needs is neither votes nor dollars but the symbolic medium of words and images. As can be seen from the dialogue between Fantine and Jean Valjean, Fantine's plea for Valjean's assistance takes the form of a direct verbal appeal. As she dies, Fantine gives Cosette over to Valjean's care with no promise to remunerate or otherwise materially compensate him. This, you may recall, is in sharp contrast to the exploitative schedule of payments extracted by the unscrupulous couple with whom she had heretofore boarded her daughter. Valjean promises Fantine that Cosette "will live within my care" and that her child "will want for nothing." In contrast to commercial and political relations, philanthropy thus acknowledges what my colleague Andrew Herman and I call "affective" rather than "effective" demand. In philanthropy, demand becomes efficacious by inviting the giver to attend primarily to the needs expressed rather than to the medium through which they are presented. Valjean's willingness to assist Fantine is philanthropy not because he is attempting to do good. Neither is it philanthropy because there is no formal legal obligation (after all, Valjean could have said no). Nor, finally, is it because his help is tax deductible or housed within the boundaries of a nonprofit organization. It is philanthropy because it is a social relation, matching resources to needs, that is mobilized and governed directly by a moral claim.

PHILANTHROPY AS SUPPLY-LED

The importance of moral claims in generating a philanthropic relation opens philanthropy, at least potentially, to a serious problem: a stark imbalance of power between donors and recipients. This arises not because philanthropists are necessarily selfish or manipulative. Rather, the moral complications of power relations arise precisely from philanthropy's being governed by moral claims. Political and commercial relations invariably retain a semblance of consumer sovereignty. They tend to be demand-led, or at least generally responsive to people's needs. In the absence of monopoly, commercial and political consumers assert a countervailing influence on the decisions of firms and politicians. The basis for this influence is the fact that consumers can meet their needs by purchase from alternative firms or support of other candidates. In contrast, philanthropic relations tend to be supply-led. Recipients possess little or no ability to "insure" or "discipline" the responsiveness of donors. This is because the producers of philanthropy are not threatened by the withdrawal of the medium for expressing a need. Appeals in the form of words and images offer no immediate extrinsic value or sanction to potential philanthropists and can, in fact, be ignored or disregarded at the immediate level of material considerations.

THE REALM OF PHILANTHROPY

One implication of the foregoing considerations is a non-institutional conception of the realm of philanthropy. As a social relation, philanthropy can exist within any sector. This is attested to, for instance, by various entrepreneurs I interviewed who insist that their special efforts to institute participatory labor practices or to offer a special quality of service for their customers is philanthropy. A similar position is held by a number of political activists in my sample. For these wealthy individuals, carrying out a heartfelt political agenda—both in the realm of electoral politics and social movements—is as philanthropic as their conventional giving. In fact, a number of activists explicitly argue that because there are no tax advantages for supporting political causes, such funding is even more philanthropic. Some who disagree with me on this point believe that calling such activity philanthropy starts us down the slippery slope leading to defining "everything" as philanthropy. That is far from my intention, however. I do maintain that every relation can be philanthropic, but only insofar as it revolves around the presentation of and response to affective, rather than effective, demand. It is also the case that this relational understanding helps resolve some of the problems plaguing sectoral definitions. For instance, care for parents, nondeductible contributions to needy individuals in or outside one's family, and attempts to stave off closing a business in order to save employees' jobs are all equally philanthropic in the sense that I have defined the term. In contrast, the institutional activity of a private school or hospital is not philanthropic just for being located in the "voluntary" or "nonprofit" sector.

WEAK CLAIMS AND STRONG RESOURCES

Much of what I have said points to the need to develop an understanding of the ethical and practical consequences of two facts: that philanthropy is resource-driven, and that recipients can make only normative claims. On the one hand, we have seen that, in the philanthropic relation, needs get communicated somewhat "weakly" as direct normative appeals rather than through the "stronger" media

91

of money or votes. On the other hand, the matching of resources and needs tends to be *supply-* rather than *demand-led*. This means that, in general, philanthropic endeavors will tend to be governed more by the availability of resources than by the existence of needs. This is not universally the case, however. Indeed, my own research and the comments of conference participants demonstrate the concern among many that philanthropy become a more reciprocal relation and even demand-led. Still, the fact remains that the "natural" or material balance of power is on the side of the giver. To take giving seriously requires that philanthropists and foundations consciously and purposefully attend to the sources of this imbalance of power and pay closer attention to the moral signals of affective demand as responsibilities as well as opportunities.

THE ETHICS OF PHILANTHROPY

At the same time that the relational definition directs attention to certain empirical workings of philanthropy, it suggests a normative criterion on which to base an ethics of philanthropy. The first question, of course, is to ask what relational considerations add to the ethics of philanthropy and how central this becomes to such an ethics. To the extent that philanthropic efforts can be evaluated on how mutual or reciprocal is the matching between gifts and needs, a number of implications for giving emerge. For instance, it becomes important to the wealthy to accord a higher priority to insuring that the needs of recipients enter into the practice of philanthropy. But even more important is the prior step of finding concrete ways to bring the moral claims of recipients more prominently into the moral horizon of givers. Perhaps Jane Addams's example of bringing the wealthy into personal contact with the needy at Hull House offers a model that can, with appropriate modification, be influential in all realms of philanthropy, from early childhood education to rehabilitation of prisoners. Ultimately, such personal contact is not at all foreign to the practice of philanthropy; it is, after all, precisely what occurs in most volunteer settings. Taking giving seriously implies a more conscious forging of the link between the giving of time and the giving of money—at least at the point when givers are deciding what to fund and what approach to take.

HUMAN FREEDOM AND THE "VOLUNTARY" NATURE OF PHILANTHROPY

I have questioned the usefulness of defining philanthropy in sectoral terms and, in particular, as the *voluntary* sector. At the same time, I have emphasized the empirical fact that the relations of philanthropy are generally governed by givers rather than recipients. If the notion of "voluntary action" is to be retained, its meaning must include the idea that philanthropy is supply-led. But there is an even more important reason for recasting the "voluntary" nature of philanthropy, namely to open consideration of the more profound issues surrounding the relation between freedom and responsibility. The ability of potential givers to disregard moral claims with less trepidation than firms and politicians can disregard dollars and votes is ultimately true only in the material realm. In the realms of spirituality, religion, and character, how one responds to moral signals is all-important.

For Valjean there is a clear and distinct duty or "moral ought" that, in an important sense, he dare not disregard. Yet it remains one of the profound ironies of human consciousness that those like Valjean, who so clearly recognize and even come to suffer from their moral duty, seem also to be those upon whom such duty weighs the least heavily. Such, for instance, is the message of Jesus's words, "My yoke is easy and my burden light." And so we see in the dialogue between Fantine and Valjean a representation of the social relation of obligation I call philanthropy. Their interaction matches the resources of a giver to the needs of a recipient on the basis of moral appeal, a realm where discussions about human freedom transcend what we conventionally mean when we refer to the voluntary nature of philanthropy. The connection of philanthropy to duty and commitment was frequently mentioned by wealthy donors in our interviews and during the conference. Nevertheless, issues of commitment, education of the wealthy to recognize their responsibilities, and the quality of the relations to recipients now too often remain at the margins of the definitions and practice of philanthropy. All this, of course, is not to turn philanthropy into moralistic arm-twisting. Rather it is to stress the invitation to commitment and the spiritual rewards revolving around the virtue of charity.

THE PRIMACY OF CHARITY IN MORAL IDENTITY

The Virtue of Charity and the Spirituality of Money

From the vantage of the foregoing considerations, we can see that philanthropy is at the point of intersection between the weakly enforced claims of those strongly in need and the strongly protected domains of those most capable of responding to such claims. Philanthropy is not simply the giving of money or time but a reciprocal social relation, one in which the needs of recipients and, indeed, the recipients themselves, make a moral claim on givers. In this view, the philanthropic response and the beginning of attention to needs within a mutual relation is contingent upon the level of moral sensitivity of givers. Much important reflection and moral education should focus on the arena of what I call the spirituality of money. At the heart of this spirituality of money and its implications for understanding the meaning and practice of money in people's lives is, simply enough, the cardinal virtue of charity. Learning what people make of money is a way to learn about what they make of philanthropy. Learning what they make of philanthropy is to learn about what they make of charity. The ethical practice of philanthropy depends in large part upon the level of moral consciousness of individual philanthropists and the quality of their bonds to recipients. In this respect, the prospects for philanthropy as a social force and as an individual commitment have much to do with revitalizing the ancient *virtue* of charity.

There is no denying that a good amount of philanthropy skirts the issues of mutuality and charity as I have outlined them to this point. In fact, it is frequently and correctly pointed out just how much of what goes as philanthropy has precious little to do with the moral primacy of charity.[2] There will, of course, always be political criteria introduced at some point into discussions about what constitutes proper philanthropic activity. Most fundamental, perhaps, is the controversy around whether philanthropy is better directed toward creating opportunities to encourage individual conversion and initiative or toward producing "structural" transformation, with the former taken as the more conservative strategy and the latter as the more liberal one. While it is certainly important to debate which of these two directions is more valuable and what specific programs and policies would do most to improve the welfare of humanity, I am persuaded that such discussions will continue long after—and perhaps even because—we decide to take giving seriously. But for now let us see at least if we can develop a broad consensus about the central social-psychological disposition that makes the specifics of philanthropy worth struggling over.

For me, the central philanthropic disposition is that of charity—what philosopher Jules Toner (1968) defines as *care*, or the dedicated attention to love others in their true needs. Care is the practical or "implemental" side of *radical love*. Toner defines radical love as the irreducible affection by which a lover "affirms the beloved for the beloved's self (as a radical end). . . [and] by which the lover affectively identifies with the loved one's personal being, by which in some sense the lover is the beloved affectively" (p. 183). Care, then, says Toner, "is an affirmative affection toward someone precisely as in need. It is not the need nor what is needed that is the object of radical care; radical care is of the one who has the need, under the aspect of needing. For example, I have an affection of care toward one who needs food or friendly words or a listener or instruction. As a consequence of care, I desire food for him, or friendly words and so on. If I have a care or concern for the food or words or instruction, etc. it is only. . . relative and derivative care," not radical care (p. 75).

There are certainly many terms to ponder even in these careful definitions. What precisely is an "affirmative affection"? What are the true needs of others? How do people, much less *we*, know their needs? And even then, what is to be done to meet these needs? The list of questions is endless, even though Toner goes a long way toward answering many of them in his persuasive book. For now, however, let us see if we can agree that to speak of taking giving seriously is properly to search for the ideal in regard to the orientation and identity of a philanthropist, that is, to agree, at least for the moment, that *caritas* is the fundamental starting point for any serious discussion of serious giving and ultimately for those abiding questions concerning the philosophy, politics, and policy of giving.

Bringing Charity Back In

To rekindle the discussion of charity is, as I have said, to emphasize issues of self-identity. But self-identity needs to be understood in a more profound way than it is in modern discourse. The modern notion of self-identity focuses on the individual as the center of moral consciousness and moral decision. Bellah and associates (1985) speak of the utilitarian, biblical, civic, and expressive varieties of individualism. In each variety, a different set of ambiguities arises surrounding the perennial problem of bridging the gulf between personal fulfillment and public involvement. Admittedly it is hard to concoct a formula to supplant this dualism, but, in point of fact, many of those interviewed in the course of their study "evince an individualism that is not empty but is full of content drawn from an active identification with communities and traditions" (p. 163). In examining this non-antithetical orientation, Bellah and associates turn mainly to the civic traditions of citizenship and voluntary association. I want to suggest a different language for dealing with the ambiguities of self-identity, one that draws on the meaning of charity as love. Such an approach has its own problems, mainly revolving around the fact that the discourse of love is not as prominent a part of the American cultural heritage as are the notions of citizenship and civic responsibility. Still, I hope what may be lost initially in being unable to address the language of love to a wide audience may be offset in the end by the profound attraction of the vocation of charity. If the modern sense of self-identity stresses *self*, the reconceptualization of the virtue of charity stresses *identity*.

Emphasizing the notion of self-*identity* as the basis for *self*-identity is at the heart of the Thomistic concept of love, or charity. Although Thomas Aquinas did not speak of identity, his concept of love does presume an understanding of identification: by the fact that love transforms the lover into the beloved, it makes the lover enter inside the beloved, and the converse, so that there is nothing of the beloved that is not united to the lover, just as the form attains the innermost recesses of that which it informs, and conversely (in III Sent., d 27, q. 1, a. 1, ad 4., as cited by Gilleman 1959, p. 126).

Such a formulation would be foreign to Jean Valjean, but the underlying sentiments are not. Ironically, in the late-modern period in which we live, the formula may be more readily embraced than the sentiments. In this era when self-development is a purposive, reflective activity for many, we hear a lot about "creative selfishness," along with the more classical phrase of Tocqueville, "self-interest rightly understood." Such notions are bothersome to many because they provide such a wide opening for justifying one's individual or group interests as the common good. But the existence of this temptation does not undercut the valid underpinnings of the idea that the fullest morality accompanies an appreciation of identity of interests. One reaction to our contemporary culture's profession of a self-serving version of community of interests, say, between giver and recipients, is an attempt to purify the motives of givers by calling for various strategies of disinterestedness, altruism, and anonymity on behalf of donors. Curiously, such approaches of selflessness are offered as remedies precisely in that area of spiritual and financial devotedness in which the quality of self and self-identity, rather than selflessness, is what mobilizes and sustains commitment. If there is one thing to be learned from my interviews with millionaires and from the discussions at the conference, it is that any strategy of purification of motivation should be directed not toward convincing donors of the disinterestedness of charity but toward strengthening inner convictions about the sensitivity, intensity, extent, and insight of their identifications with those in need. This, suggests Thomas, is precisely the basis for that paradoxical unity between duty and pleasure (satisfaction), which the most committed donors cite as the linchpin of their giving:

> Love always supposes a complacency of the lover in the beloved. Now when someone takes pleasure in another, he transports himself into that other and joins himself to him as far as possible, so that the other becomes his own; that is why love has the property of uniting lover and beloved (in I Sent., d. 10, q. 1, a. 3., as cited by Gerard Gilleman 1959, p. 126).

In his treatise on charity, Gilleman (1959) explicitly addresses the problem that Thomas's understanding leaves open the possibility that, in the name of love, one may end up being either egocentric or altruistic. This is because Thomas asserts both the primacy of free will and the fact that any evaluation of an act of love has both an objective and a subjective component. Objectively, it is always appropriate to ask whether, in fact, a professed intention of charity actually accomplishes its desired end. Still, the very possibility of inquiring about the value of objective outcomes and of calling individuals to accountability derives from establishing the goal of love as the common starting point. To concede the norm of love is to admit much; for in doing so we acknowledge a crucial subjective criterion for evaluating practical judgments. Clearly, the virtue of charity does not guide every philanthropic decision. Equally important, it is never possible for one person to judge whether another's philanthropy conforms to the dictates of charity. Nevertheless, establishing the "primacy of charity" remains important. For doing so provides the basis for establishing the ideal of philanthropy as a social relation and the basis for individuals to judge their own efforts. Ultimately, moving charity to center stage obviates concerns about the contaminating influence of self-love and shifts the emphasis to the relation between love of self and love of neighbor. As Gilleman says, "For St. Thomas there is no place in a morally good act of will for an absolute disjunction between love referred to self and love referred to another. The proper effect of love is to associate self with the other" (1959, p. 125).

With this in mind, we can see the significance of defining philanthropy as the social relation in which we extend our self-interest to include meeting the needs of others. Philanthropy, as one of many important defining acts of self, is the relationship in which we directly attend to and respond to noncoercive, *affective* (rather than effective) expressions of need. The implication is that for such charity to be caring, rather than controlling or self-aggrandizing, some personal knowledge of the object of love is necessary. The philanthropist in stewardship must, like Isaiah's suffering servant, "know our sorrows and be acquainted with grief." According to Gilleman, this is why, for Thomas, love "must be conceived as communion between persons, that is, an act by which one affectively associates another with himself and wishes that the resulting unity be perfectly accomplished in a common and identical happiness" (p. 125). Despite the high moral tone of these words, we hear them echoed as both ideal and reality in the comments of many wealthy persons who already strive to take giving seriously. In noting this, we must never forget that the call to charity is not the preserve of the wealthy. The nonwealthy too are implicated in and respond to this same vocation of charity.

Socialization to Charity

The foregoing analysis of what it means for the wealthy to "take giving seriously" points toward a number of specific implications for elevating the moral quality of philanthropy among those who are already predisposed to substantial giving and for instilling such dedication in others. Defining philanthropy as a social relation of *caritas* suggests that efforts to improve the quality of philanthropy among the wealthy, including increasing their generosity, entails a two-fold attention to the issue of self-identity. On the one hand, we must see philanthropy as a matter of *self*-development among donors; to become a serious giver means to conceptualize oneself in a new way. On the other, it means expanding the horizons of care within which donors experience an obligation of identification, a vocation of communion, with other human beings as radical ends.

It will come as no surprise that as a sociologist examining the issue of moral biography, I emphasize the importance of the simple yet crucial notion of socialization as the key to advancing the development of this two-pronged strategy. Such socialization, we have observed, is critical to the identity-formation process of the serious givers who participated in the conference. Presumably, socialization is equally important for extending an identity of serious philanthropy to their peers, and to their daughters and sons. Within the discourse of moral biography and vocation in which I have couched my analysis, identity-formation entails vocation, vocation entails conversion, conversion entails socialization, and socialization entails relationship. Both taking giving seriously and the path to that responsibility are ultimately a matter of social relations. But taking giving seriously is not just any vocation. It is a specific set of social relations in which one becomes dedicated to a communion of interests with others such that attention to their needs is a form of radical love.

Thanks to Howard S. Becker's ([1960] 1970) illuminating article, "Notes on the Concept of Commitment," I am able to be more precise about what the vocation of philanthropy entails. Becker's phenomenology of commitment is an effort to describe what is entailed in becoming dedicated to what he calls "consistent lines of activity," meaning a sustained level of concern over time. This means getting beyond the tautological proposition that "commitment produces consistent lines of activity" (p. 265). The conceptual innovation that Becker introduces to locate the elusive factor that underlies commitment is the notion of a "side bet." "The committed person has acted in such a way as to involve other interests of his—originally extraneous to the action he is engaged in—directly in that action. By his own actions prior to the final bargaining session, he has staked something of value to him, something originally unrelated to this present line of action, on being consistent in his present behavior" (p. 266). It is easy to see the side bets and how they are enforced in the commercial and political relations I have described previously. In both cases, consistency of behavior in a current business or political transaction is reinforced by the countervailing power of the consumer to withdraw future material support. Here the side bet by the executive and the politician is their dependence on future support. Any failure to perform according to expectations in the current situation threatens the forfeiture of future dealings. In philanthropy, however, there are no material side bets by the donor. There are material contributions of time and effort, but any side bets that insure commitment remain in the moral realm— for example, guilt, the loss of self-esteem, the threat to public status, the reduction of personal satisfaction, the violation of principles, and, in some cases, a breach in the relationship with God. Ultimately, any "side benefit" revolves around what the philanthropist regards to be a sustained moral interest. Ideally—and that is how we must speak in the realm of charity—the only moral interest worthy of philanthropic commitment is one that is materially unenforceable: the value of the recipients and their needs. In this view, then, taking giving seriously means taking steps to raise the needs of others to the level of a sustained interest of the donor.

Given this relational framework, the practical implication is to encourage at every opportunity the kinds of interactions that educate to charity those who are currently wealthy as well as those who are becoming wealthy—through business or inheritance. It is, in effect, a matter of creating a sensitivity about what side bets are important. Based on the foregoing analysis, the focus on moral identity and social interaction implies, first, the need to elaborate strategies that will induce the wealthy to be more attentive to the moral signals of affective demand, as they are enunciated by and on behalf of those in need. Second, this means initiating ways in which the wealthy may come in contact not only with the needs of recipients but with the recipients themselves. Third, this means assisting the wealthy in their efforts to both find and create appropriate organizational vehicles and personal practices for carrying out their moral vocation in the realm of philanthropy.

In particular, to instill a dedication to serious giving means making the foregoing philosophical and theoretical directions the basis for introducing wealthy individuals to each of the six mobilizing factors [See Chapter 1.] that shape a philanthropic identity. As I have indicated, each of the six variables is important, both for introducing and for reinforcing a commitment to charity. If any single piece of practical advice emerges from this essay, it is that taking giving seriously results from taking the *giver* seriously. The key is to encircle the potential giver within a community of peers who serve as mentors. These peers must appreciate the hesitancies and aspirations of the wealthy person. But they also must have experienced the rewarding identity of giving enough to, sometimes gently and sometimes forcefully, stretch the identity of the potential donor. These peers must *ask* their associate, friend, or child to experiment with them in the realm of philanthropy, to "taste and see" the experience of *caritas*.

At the same time, the wealthy must be encircled by a community of need—their own as well as that of others. Ironically enough, the greatest incentive to develop a moral identity of care may be the profound needs of the wealthy rather than simply their response to the needs of others. What Mother Teresa told Fred about the great loneliness of the affluent may ultimately prove to be the greatest incentive to serious philanthropy. "People perish without a vision," remarks Fred. They also, we have heard, perish in isolation. So many in the world, says David, "have lost the agency to seek inward and outward life for every individual. They are so alone and unable to change their circumstances—and this is true not just for people in poverty." It is philanthropy as the extension of one's horizons of identification and as a response to the needs of others, valued as radical ends, that enables the wealthy to ease—for themselves and others—what Dorothy Day calls "the long loneliness."

Notes

1. I am grateful to Susan Ostrander for working out many of the ideas in this section with me (see Ostrander and Schervish, 1990). I take responsibility for whatever questions readers may raise about adding the notion of "charity" to our original formulation of philanthropy as a social relation. The bulk of this section is a revised version of a paper (Schervish, 1988) presented at the 1988 Independent Sector Academic Retreat in Indianapolis.

2. Teresa Odendahl's *Charity Begins at Home* (1990), Alan Rabinowitz's *Social Change Philanthropy* (1990), and Robert F. Arnove's *Philanthropy and Cultural Imperialism* (1980), to name only a few articulate critiques, all warn against the particularly strong temptations for philanthropy to be self-serving on both a personal and an institutional level.

Bibliography

Arnove, Robert F. (Ed.). 1980. *Philanthropy and Cultural Imperialism: The Foundations at Home and Abroad.* Bloomington: Indiana University Press.

Becker, Howard S. [1960] 1970. "Notes on the Concept of Commitment." Chapter 18 in *Sociological Work.* Chicago: Aldine.

Bellah, Robert N., Richard Madsen, William M. Sullivan, Ann Swidler, and Steven M. Tipton. 1985. *Habits of the Heart: Individualism and Commitment in American Life.* New York: Harper and Row.

Gilleman, S.J., Gerard. 1959. *The Primacy of Charity in Moral Theology.* Westminster, Maryland: The Newman Press.

Odendahl, Teresa. 1990. *Charity Begins at Home: Generosity and Self-Interest Among the Philanthropic Elite.* New York: Basic Books.

Ostrander, Susan A. and Paul G. Schervish. 1990. "Giving and Getting: Philanthropy as a Social Relation." Jon Van Til (Ed.), *Critical Issues in American Philanthropy: Strengthening Theory and Practice.* San Francisco: Jossey-Bass.

Payton, Robert L. 1991. "Philanthropy in a Liberal Education: A Discussion Paper." Indiana University Center on Philanthropy. Indiana University-Purdue University at Indianapolis.

Rabinowitz, Alan. 1990. *Social Change Philanthropy in America.* New York: Quorum Books.

Schervish, Paul G. 1988. "Bringing Recipients Back In: Philanthropy as a Social Relation." Independent Sector Academic Retreat. Indianapolis. June 7-8.

_____. 1991. "The Sound of One Hand Clapping: The Dialectic or Care and Control in Anonymous Giving." Conference on Anonymous Giving. Indiana University Center on Philanthropy. Indianapolis. February 6-8.

Schervish, Paul G. and Andrew Herman. 1988. *Final Report: The Study on Wealth and Philanthropy.* Social Welfare Research Institute. Boston College. Chestnut Hill, Massachusetts.

Toner, Jules. 1968. *The Experience of Love.* Washington, D.C.: Corpus Book.

Van Til, Jon. 1990. "Defining Philanthropy." Jon Van Til (Ed.), *Critical Issues in American Philanthropy: Strengthening Theory and Practice.* San Francisco: Jossey-Bass.

INDEX

A

Aquinas, St. Thomas, 97

Addams, Jane, 92

administration, 16-19

    foundation advantages and disadvantages, 17-18

Ahmanson Foundation, 72

alternative community chest, 52-53

alternative funds, 74-75

Annenberg Foundation, 72

anonymity

    reasons for and against, 20-21

    versus recognition, 19-22

ARF (amalgamated rich folks), 75

B

baby boomers, 73-75, 78

    wealth, 68-69

Becker, Howard S., 100

Bellah, Robert N., 96

Benton Foundation, 72

Benz, Obie, 1, 43

Boisi, Geoffrey T., 30

boundaries of philanthropy, 5-6

C

Cambridge College, 63-64

caritas. See charity

Carnegie Foundation, 72

charity, 96-102

    primacy in moral identity, 94-96

    self-identity, 96-97

    socialization towards, 99-102

    virtue, 12, 94-96

Charter Fund, 18

children

    deprived upbringing, 43-44

    educating in philanthropy, 27

    innovative philanthropy, 28-29

Children of Crisis, 67

civil pluralism, 24

Coles, Robert, 67

Index

collective donor groups, 52
commerce, different from philanthropy and politics, 88-89
community of participation, 33, 38-39
Cornell University's Department of Economics and Housing, 68

D

Day, Dorothy, 102
directed distribution, 50-51
disposable resources, 36, 38
donors, intrinsic vs. extrinsic benefits, 7
Dulany, Peggy, 2, 59
Duvivier-Gary, Tracy, 76

E

early childhood experience, 34, 38, 59-62
Ellman, Benjamin, 38-40
ethics, 92
evolving processes, 63-64
extrinsic benefits of philanthropic activity, 7

F

Federal Reserve Board, 69
Ford Foundation, 24, 72
foundations, 52, 72
    advantages, 18
    disadvantages, 17-18
    traditional industry support, 72
    women's, 76
framework of consciousness, 33-34, 39-40, 59-60
Funding Exchange, 43, 75
funds, alternative, 74-75

G

Gillman, S. J., 98
good self, 22-26
good society, 22-26
    philanthropic contributions, 24
government assistance, 8-9
Greeley, Andrew, 28

H

Haymarket Foundation, 52-53
Herman, Andrew, 90
Hewlett-Packard Foundation, 72
Hughes Foundation, 72
human freedom and voluntary philanthropy, 93-94

Index

P

Index